Dedicated
to
Lawrence D. Heath

Your commitment and strength in your profession and family is a standard to which I still aspire.

Concrete Wedding Cake

What I have learned
about
motion picture editing
and other stuff.

By
John Heath

Table of Contents

Background Noise

Follow the Story and Lead the Audience

For Directors Only

Background Noise

My Cinematic
Biography
Resume and Genealogy

I am third generation to the motion picture business. My grandfather, Frank Heath, was a part of the very beginnings of the film industry in New York. He worked through the transition from the "Silent Era" to "The Talkies" finishing his career at Warner Bros. as an assistant director on some of their biggest pictures during the 1940s.

My father, Lawrence Heath, was an editor starting in the early days of television working on *The Burns and Allen Show*. He worked in films and television into the 1990s. He was the first of my teachers and mentors.

Dad with George Burns on *The Burns and Allen Show* in the 1950s

My Grandfather, Frank Heath, on the left, working in New York in the 1920s with director Edwin Hollywood, who by the way never made it in Hollywood

As a boy, I would visit and spend time with my father while he worked in the cutting room. In my teens, I worked for him as an apprentice, splicing film and running errands during the summer. I was exposed to the process of film editing when it was a very physical, as well as, creative process. Editors used Moviolas for viewing and marking the film with grease pencils. They cut the film with scissors, and spliced with Bell and Howell hot splicers. Film was on reels, and synchronizers were used to keep the picture and sound in sync. All of which are museum artifacts now but were the tools of the trade then. The process and tools had a great deal to do with the style of editing just as Avid or Final Cut have affected editing today.

The business of Motion Pictures is as much about time and money as it is about the creative process. When viewing films of the past, it's important to consider that the look and feel of them is as much about the limitations of the tools used as it is the about the abilities of those making the films. In those days, up until digital editing became practical, editors worked in film with one picture and one sound track. Except for an occasional sound effect like a gun shot to sweeten a scene or a mono music track to cut a montage, the editor's job was to cut a single track of dialogue synced to one track of spliced picture. Today, with multiple tracks for sound and for picture, the editor's creative choices have greatly expanded but so have his responsibilities.

I started when film was still being used. My first Union-paying job" was with Metromedia Producers Corp. I was given the glamorous job of reclaiming fill leader from sound effects mixing units. I was put in a windowless room filled with boxes to the ceiling. A tedious job, but I was grateful to be taking home $85.00 a week. One day, Tom Walsh, then an assistant editor, was backed up and came to my room to ask if I knew how to sync dailies. Having never done it before, I said "Sure." With only a few missteps, I figured it out. What it did give me though was the opportunity to watch the work of editor John Martinelli. I never went back to that room with all those boxes.

After that, I was an apprentice on the feature *White Buffalo* for editor Michael Anderson. I was hired to "reconstitute" dailies for Producer Dino Delaurentis to view. Because the work picture was the only copy of the film, the sequence needed to be "uncut" and reassembled in dailies form. It was a major action sequence with lots of short cuts. I think it was edited and reedited two or three times before Dino was happy .

I then became an apprentice for MTM (Mary Tyler Moore) Productions for several years where I moved up to assistant editor on the *Bob Newhart Show*, assisting   M. Pam

Blumenthal (a man). The show was shot with three cameras before an audience . The next day I would sync the film from the three cameras with a single sound track. Pam would then mark the cuts with a grease pencil on a "three headed monster," which was moviola with three picture heads coupled together to run in sync with the sound. I would splice the scenes together matching what camera angle Pam had marked on the film. It was a labor intensive process but a great way to learn how to cut comedy. Pam had his rituals. He came to work late, read the newspaper in his chair with his feet propped up on the Moviola. After he finished the paper, we would work for a few hours, and then it was time for lunch which usually lasted a few hours. He would afterward take a nap in his chair with his feet again propped up on the moviola before the afternoons work would start. Since he was a bachelor we would work late into the evening.

The first time I walked in on Pam while he was napping his eyes were open and fixed on the ceiling. I was afraid he had passed away on my first day on the job. Did I do something to kill my first editor? I walked over hesitantly touched him on the arm. He woke up with a snort, and I jumped back. He explained that he was born with eye lids that wouldn't stay up and the doctors stitched them back. He would fall asleep with his eyes shut, but they would gradually open up as he went into a deeper sleep. I never really got used to it. Pam liked to put on a gruff front, but at heart Pam was a generous man. With the support of Executive Produce Michael Zinberg, Pam offered me an episode to edit. I had to be my own assistant, but I was still excited to do it. Though not credited, it was a great experience, and I picked up valuable editing knowledge.

While I was assisting Michael Vittes on the series *Lou Grant,* I was asked to be the teaser/trailer editor on *The White Shadow*, a drama series for CBS. The trailer would be a 30 second compilation sequence from an up coming episode that would be placed at the end of an episode, starting with an announcer saying "Next on White Shadow" and would include interesting or exciting clips to entice the viewers to watch the next episode. The trailer would then become a teaser by putting it at the start of the next episode and changing the voice over to "Tonight on White Shadow." The challenge of creating an engaging exactly to the frame, 30 second piece was a great education in making the most out of the least and how parameters can enhance creativity. Many of the techniques I learned cutting trailers, I still use. Because of the tight schedule the first season of *The White Shadow,* the editor on the show, Leon Carrere, would give me scenes to edit to help out. After I cut the scenes, he would give me notes and share techniques. Later, when the show was run for the director and producers, Leon would point out which scenes I had edited. He was a very generous man and set an example of sharing and teaching the craft of editing that I have tried to follow. Ultimately leading to me writing this book.

The next season, I was promoted to my first assignment as a film editor in episodic television. The creator and executive producer was Bruce Paltrow (yes Gwyneth's dad). He and the producer/director, Mark Tinker, gave me my editing break when I was 24. Bruce was a tough and demanding boss. There were few "atta boys" and criticism was dished out without any candy coating. It was my Basic Training and like a drill instructor, he was preparing me to be a better editor. I am grateful to him for what he taught and still think of him with great fondness. I would later work with them again on *St. Elsewhere* as an editor where I was nominated by The Television Academy and by the American Cinema Editors Society for Best Editing for a Drama Series. While on *St. Elsewhere*, I got my first opportunity to direct. I directed three episodes during the last two seasons.

Cutting "old school" on St. Elsewhere in the mid 1980s

Film making from an editorial perspective is very different from that of directing. I knew that I would need to learn about working with actors and a crew if I were ever to successfully work as a director. While still an assistant editor, I studied with Tony Miller at the Film Industry Workshop to learn about acting and directing actors. Tony became a mentor and second father from whom I would often seek advice on directing and life even after I stopped studying with him. Part of Tony's *"Concept"* for acting and directing was to break down a script into its smallest and simplest elements and through his techniques of character and story analysis, reach a better understanding of the material. When I started researching for this book, I realized I could adapt some of Tony's ideas and terminology to help communicate and share my understanding of editing

I came to understand I couldn't be completely successful as a director or editor unless I understood the writer's intent for story, the behavior of the characters, the director's vision and the techniques to flesh them out for the screen .

What I appreciated most about Tony's concept was not only how it gave me a technique to make choices but also a terminology to critique and improve a performance.

While finishing up the sixth and final season of *St. Elsewhere,* producer and director Scott Brazil, whose career spanned from *Hill Street Blues* to *The Shield,* asked me to join him as a producer and director on a new show he was producing for GTG (Grant Tinker's production company) and CBS called *TV 101*. TV 101 was a show about a high school broadcast news class. We were one of the first shows to intercut amateur video with film. It was also the first show that I worked on that edited on a nonlinear video editing system. It was called the CMX 6000.The editors cut from of laser discs as the source. At the time the majority of television shows were still being cut on film It was a challenge, but also great fun making it up as we went along. Scott was a friend from when I was an apprentice editor at MTM, and he was a production assistant. Later, I would go on to produce and direct with Scott on two more series, *WIOU* and *Jack's Place.* Scott was a great mentor when it came to the craft of producing episodic television as well as a great friend.

I later edited on the sitcom *Major Dad* for John Stephens and Earl Pomerantz. *Major Dad* was the first time I worked as an editor with my dad . He was the associate producer and he asked me to cut the pilot episode of *Major Dad.* It had an extremely short schedule. It was to be shot with four cameras twice before an audience on a Thursday night. The schedule called for us to deliver to the network, a finished, complete sound mix, color corrected, titled, with an original score, master, on the next Wednesday. From the time the dailies came in the next morning until delivery to the network I was never off the clock. I'm pretty sure that turn around is a record that no one has matched. On Sunday morning, I ran the first cut with the director and the producers in a cramped cutting room.

While I was working on making a change the director had asked for I noticed the edit list on the monitor disappear. I looked to my assistant (and future editor) Augie Hess, who had also seen the same thing. Two days and nights of work seemed to be lost. Not being tech savvy, the rest of the room was oblivious. After a moment, Augie coolly said "I think it's time for a break," and the crowd left the room for coffee and restroom breaks. Augie was able to restore the list and the show. For a few minutes though, I did experience a feeling of dread. Not only would I need to redo all the work, it would have been a great disappointment for my dad who had trusted me to make this schedule work. I later when on to edit on *LA Law* for Steven Bochco, *Picket Fences* for David Kelley, and then *Book of Daniel* and *Warehouse 13* for Jack Kenny. I also produced and directed on the series *Chicago Hope* for David Kelley, John Tinker, Bill D'Elia and James Hart and on *The Guardian* for David Hollander, Michael Pressman and Vahan Moosekian.

The transition from film to digital editing in the 90s, was painful but still exciting. To survive and remain competitive, editors were forced to learn awkward, nonlinear systems using *Laser discs,* VHS or Beta tapes. To be honest, none of the systems were as quick or as easy to use as film until we started working digitally. However, it was a necessary process to get to where we are today with Avid and Final Cut Pro.

One of the early systems was developed jointly through CBS and Sony. I was about to start as a film editor on the first season of St. Elsewhere when I was asked by the studio to "test drive" the system. The film dailies from *St. Elsewhere* were transferred to tape for me to cut. The *St. Elsewhere pilot* was troubled from the beginning. It was shut down after the first week of shooting for major recasting and the director was replaced. When I came on to do the test, there had been reshoots and the producers had been working and reworking the pilot with the editor for many months in the cutting room. There may not be anything more stressful than getting new show off the ground in its first season. Since I had worked with the same producers on White Shadow, I can remember being disappointed that I wasn't asked originally to cut the pilot. *I understand now though, they wanted someone with more experience.* Since I was just testing the system, I edited the pilot with no input or notes from the producers or director. I worked quietly, most of the time it was just me and the engineer who was working on the test to make sure the equipment ran smoothly . When I finished editing the test I dropped off a tape copy of the show to the producer's office as a "FYI the system worked fine." Several of the producers, I suppose out of curiosity, decided to watch the tape. Well they like what they saw, and the next week all the dailies and the reels from the pilot were brought to my cutting room and I was the editor for the Pilot of St. Elsewhere.   I think I had the advantage of being outside the center of the storm as I put the show together. It's an example of how important it is to be objective and to stay the audience when working on a project. *St. Elsewhere* was the first of several projects I was asked to re-edit.

Throughout my years of producing, directing and editing, I have been involved with a lot of editing. Much of it my own but even more done by others. From an editor's first cut to a final locked picture, I have participated in all stages of editing including director, producer, studio and network versions.

I have seen a lot of well crafted innovative editing. I have also seen editing that was awkward, confusing, and tedious. Aside from bad technique, the worst editing I've seen usually has unmotivated cuts and confusing structure. I often asked myself, why would these editors make such unsuccessful editorial choices. While many editors seem to have a naturally good sense of how to construct a clear and entertaining motion picture, others clearly need a structure, terminology and process to approach the work.

Feeling I could draw upon my experience to come up with an approach for quality editing, I was motivated to write this book. My goal is to share, with those who want to learn about editing and become better editors, by illustrating the techniques and approaches I have learned that constitute an effective editorial process. I will share what I have learned of editing from my father and the other editors whom I assisted. I'll explain the way I cut and what I have discovered through my own trial and error. During my career, I have received great tips and advice. I have worked with great producers and directors who have given notes that showed me how I could be a better editor. In preparing this book, I looked for what I could bring from my experience in a practical and light approach that is neither overly technical nor too theoretical.

Follow the Story and Lead the Audience

Theories, Techniques, and Advice
on
Motion Picture Editing
as
I Understand It

I

"Oh, you're an editor."

"Oh, you're an editor. So you take out all the mistakes the actors make..... I just love those bloopers." I know people that judge editing based on the errors in continuity. Most editors have heard these kinds of remarks when asked at a party "so, what do you do?" Then as you try to explain the job it only confuses people more. Most understand what a writer does, and they generally understand what a director does, but very few have any understanding of what an editor actually does. There is no sense of romance associated with editing as compared to a writer struggling with the creative process or the adventure of a director commanding a set and crew. The image of an editor is that of a lonely vitamin D deficient figure hunched over a monitor tediously toiling away. And the truth is, it's a pretty accurate depiction. My early editing sessions were usually fueled with coffee and cigarettes in the morning. In the afternoon and evening it was Coke (the soft drink) and cigarettes. I no longer smoke and I've switched to Diet Pepsi.

Editing is a difficult solitary job that can be made frustrating and infuriating when dealing with the shortcomings of the script or production. I once heard an editor say when asked how were the dailies, "Today's dailies were a concrete wedding cake"... beautiful to look at but impossible to cut." I must admit that editorial humor tends to be negative and cynical. The point is that no matter how interesting the cinematography or inspired the acting, if the director doesn't understand the fundamentals of film making the movie's potential may never be realized because it can't be properly edited.

Another reason for cynicism is that editing usually goes unnoticed when done well. There are some smart creative people in the business who appreciate what an editor does, and it is great to work with them. However, for the most part, editors must learn to be secure in their ability and take satisfaction in knowing the best possible work has been done. To do this, you must learn the craft of editing and be available to continuing to learn. It's important to be able to criticize your work. Editing is re-editing. Back when I cut on film, I would put a scene that I had just cut on the rack to "let it age" for a couple of days. It was always a different scene when I viewed it later. Some problems disappeared, while others would pop up. Because of this it's important to allow time to go through your work before anyone sees it. With a **First Cut,** you express how the you feel the story should play. This is why it's important to do the best possible representation of the story based on the script with guidance from the director. Never screen a "Rough Cut", A term my father never used, that should be offensive to every editor.

What Editing Is

Editing is the convergence of all the aspects of a motion picture. The writer brings the story, the actors breath life into the characters, with the director guiding how the audience will experience the motion picture. It is the task of the editor to bring these elements together in the most effective way to create **the motion picture the writer and director intended.** The writer's and then the director's intent is primary to the editorial decision making process. So, pardon me, in advance, if I restate this point several times.

In general, I think editing should be transparent to the audience. If the motion picture is engaging and entertaining, chances are it was well edited. First, you're given the story and its elements in the script. The script describes the events, the characters' dialogue and actions in sequences or scenes.

The characters' **dialogue** furthers the plot, affects the relationships or reveals aspects of the characters. Through the words of the story, the writer creates **Ideas** that are conveyed in each **moment** of the story. In a sense, editing is choosing how best to communicate these ideas.

The emotions and feelings that the actors bring to the dialogue and action also advance the story and further the understanding of the characters. The actors create unspoken ideas through emotion, facial expressions, physical behavior and body language. The movement and the physical actions of the actors advance the story or the understanding of the characters. These actions can be scripted, directed, actor choices or spontaneous reactions. Understanding these movements is important because **so much of editing is motivated and driven by movement.**

To make informed editorial choices, you first must have an understanding of the writer's intent and the director's vision of the movie for each moment and each sequence.

You're provided the story through the performances and the director's visual interpretation. It is photographed from various angles and compositions from wide to close, and the sound is recorded to create the **coverage** for each scene.

As the editor you guide the story that the audience will experience through each moment and sequence of the motion picture by **choosing the perspective** from all the sights and sound choices available .

II

The Editor's Cut

I learned editing the way I learned English. I grew up around it. I didn't learn how to diagram a sentence until fourth grade in Sister Amie's class. I learned editing by example as I was growing up and then as an apprentice and assistant editor. After I started editing, I continued to learn by doing. I was blessed with having pretty good editorial instincts, but I couldn't always explain why I cut a scene a certain way. I can remember being asked by a director, "why did you cut there?" and not having a good answer except that "it felt right." As I gained experience, it was clear I needed to have an understanding and terminology, so I could grow as an editor and work better with others. Someone who wants to be an editor not only needs to learn editing techniques but also how to creatively approach the work. Below, I believe is the first and constant question that the you need to ask when editing.

"What is <u>most important</u> for the audience to see and /or hear, <u>at this moment</u>, that best tells the story?"

Knowing the intent and point of a scene, knowing what motivates and drives the actors and knowing the director's vision are the only ways to understand and completely answer this question. It's the nature of editing that you're constantly making value judgments." Understanding the story and characters behavior is the only way to make informed choices using creativity and intelligence to present the best possible Editor's Cut. The challenge in editing is remaining focused on the story that needs to be told. Much of editing is problem solving. The nature of the process is to constantly come up against roadblocks that hinder the choices you want to make. The timing of camera moves or action may be different from take to take. The actor may have different movements from one angle to the next at the point in the scene where the editor wishes to make a cut. Frustration is the most common emotion. What you can't forget is that it's the editor role by using craft, intelligence, and creativity to make sure that the story is told in a clear and engaging way.

Editorial Interpretation

In narrative motion pictures there is a **reliance on interpretation** by the audience for a complete understanding of the story. This includes the most important ideas and aspects of the story, along with the expositional information. You're making choices from the **palette of the sights and sounds** available, to inform and guide the audience's attention to follow the story. So remember, **for each idea of each moment** that is expressed by the actor and filmed by the director, the editor influences the story's understanding by **choosing the perspective of how each moment is seen and heard by the audience.** Your goal is to choose the **perspective that best communicates the idea intended by the writer** for each moment of the story.

My Take

I've stated what I think editing is and what your goals as an editor should be. With the rest of the book, I hope to help you achieve those goals. I will discuss terminology, theories and techniques that I have learned or developed over my years of experience in and around editing. I will give you advice about editing. Much of what I say may be a place to start rather than the final word. I will discuss what's worked for me, how editorial choices can affect the audiences' understanding and appreciation of the story, and how to help you be a more creative and effective editor.

III
The Cut, The Cut and The Cut

To start with a basic, for clear communication in the cutting room, an editor uses the term "Cut" in several contexts. The action of the motion picture is photographed in a series of still frames, usually at 24 frames per second. The first use of the term "cut" refers to any **one of a series of shots of specific action that are edited together that make up a sequence.** An example, "I think we can drop the third cut in this sequence."

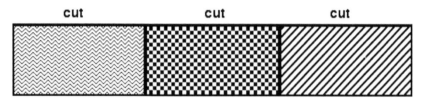

A **sequence** may be a single scene from the script, or it may be multiple scenes that work together as a specific part of the story with a natural beginning and end.

The **first frame of the action of the shot is the "Head"** of the cut, and the **last frame is the "Tail"** of the cut. **"Cut"** is also used to describe the instantaneous transition from the **"tail" or end** of one shot to the **"head"** or beginning of another shot. Used as in " I think you can trim a few frames off the head of that cut." or "add a beat to the tail of that cut."

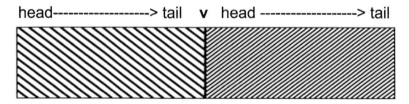

The end of the cut is also referred to as the **"A side"** of the cut. The beginning of the cut or head of the cut is called the **"B side"** of the of the transition. As in " If you add a few frames to A side of that cut, you get a better match."

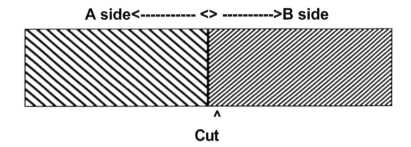

A side<----------- <> ---------->B side

^
Cut

The cut, as a transition, may be seamless as a continuation of an action or an idea. It can also be a transition to new information, as for example, cutting from one setting at the end of a sequence to a new setting for the next.

The last use of the term **"Cut"** in the cutting room is as a version of the completed work,as in **The First Cut, The Director's Cut or The Final Cut.** Understanding these terms and their context is important to clearly communicate editing concepts and ideas when working in the cutting room.

IV

Put Some Steak on That Sizzle

Editing with energy that is visually dazzling is fun, but if it's without interesting and engaging content, it can be as satisfying as cotton candy. Most of us have experienced looking at a cloud and finding shapes that make us recall familiar objects or beings. Humans are largely visual beings who tend to see patterns when trying to make sense of what is before them. This phenomenon is called Pareidolia. In motion pictures, the audience is following the **editor's cutting pattern.** Each picture cut builds on the previous to create a visual pattern for the audience to follow during each sequence. In making editing choices, the editor must have fidelity to the story and characters' development.

Again, the editor should ask, **"What is most important for the audience to see and/or hear from moment to moment to communicate each idea of the story?"**

The audience's understanding and interpretation of each cut is influenced by what cut comes before and after. A logical order to the sights and sounds of the motion picture is critical. The editing pattern is analogous to grammar in writing. If the "syntax" of the cutting pattern is off, so will the comprehension and appreciation of the motion picture's story. **If every important idea** that is necessary for the story is not included, the editor's cutting pattern will create confusion by not giving the audience everything needed to understand the story. Conversely, **showing more than what is necessary** to inform the story or character development may be misleading.

Follow the Story and Lead the Audience

Because of the requirements of production scheduling, editing is usually done in sequences that have been shot out of script order. So, in preparation to cut, the editor should distill the sequence down to its most basic story elements to understand what is most important to be seen, heard and accomplished in the scene. When selecting a sequence to edit, I will usually grab the one earliest in script order if possible.

Until you gain experience, it may help to write a short synopsis for the sequence. With this the editor should have a guide to **lead the audience** to what is needed to be seen and heard, what each character needs to accomplish, as well as what is the meaning and point of the scene. This synopsis can also be used for the continuity in the breakdown of the whole movie.

The truth is nobody on the production team has a more intimate relationship with the film than the editor. However, unlike the writer who chooses the words or the director who supervises the creation of the imagery, the editor is given the elements and asked to tell the story.

Major Breakdown

Editing is an interpretive craft. Along with understanding the story and the writer's intent, the editor must also understand the visual style and emotional spirit by which the director wishes to present the story. If not clear on these, the editor will be handicapped from fully fleshing out the story. The editor should be a part of story or tone meetings. If not invited, the editor should ask if it's possible to participate. Personally, whenever I have had problems with editing on a project, it was due to either my lack of complete understanding of the writers or directors intention or their lack of clarity in communicating it. In preparation of editing, the script should be broken-down.

As the **assistant director** breaks down the script for the purpose of budget and scheduling production. The editor and assistant should break down the script into story, character and transitional elements. The assistant editor should prepare a **continuity.** A continuity is a list of all the scenes of the script in a spreadsheet format. It should list each scene with its number. It should include the characters, along with a short description of each scene's action and finally, a column for each scene's timing. The continuity should also list any transitional pieces such as establishing shots that are scripted. Later as scenes are edited, the timing of each scene should be added to the continuity. This will be a useful document throughout the editorial process. The first version of the continuity can be prepared with extra space in the "scene description" area for the editor's use to make notes when prepping the script .

The first step is to just read the script. **Don't try to analyze the story.** If something bumps or jumps out that raises a question, make a note. Next read each scene and ask some basic questions, using the "5 Ws," who, what, when, where, and why. Make notes on a copy of the continuity to use in any story meetings with the writer and/or director. **Don't be afraid to ask questions.** I have been in story meetings where the number of different interpretations of a story point matched the number of people in the room. The nature of scripts is that there is a minimum description of the action and subtext. Being clear on the points in the beginning helps later on during editing.

As new versions of the script come out, read them for how the changes will affect your understanding of the script. Instead of anyone else, the editor should replace the pages. That will insure that all the revisions have been seen. Again, it's not uncommon for there to be misunderstandings or differences in understandings of the script. That is why it's important to include the editor in story and tone meetings to insure "everyone is on the same page."

If being a part of these meetings is impossible, and the director is unavailable to answer any questions, the editor may answer questions with a story and character analysis. An analysis of the story's situations and of the characters' behavior can be done for a better understanding.

For example, character John enters Bob's cutting room. Bob scolds John for how he did the editing changes in Act Two. John reacts with anger and yells at Bob. There is an awkward beat between them. Then John storms out. Bob is left standing there stunned.

The setting is Bob's cutting room. What does the setting say about their relationship? Bob didn't go to John's cutting room to confront him. Bob asked John to come to him which is a place where Bob is in a more powerful position. You may assume Bob is John's boss. You could assume that either they don't have a close personal relationship or, if they did, it is strained.

John yelled at Bob after being scolded. Bob doesn't say anything. He doesn't yell back or fire John. You could assume the Bob's power or authority is compromised, otherwise he would yell back or fire John. Why John is disrespectful will probably be revealed in the story. What is clear, is that John is not concerned with the consequences of yelling at Bob.

This kind of analysis can help in editing choices. When the audience needs to see the listener or see the speaker? How long should a reaction cut be?

When should a pause be created? Bob's reaction to being yelled at by John is different in type and length if it's the first time it's happened or if it is common in their relationship.

While a simplistic example, it demonstrates how you can reach a better understanding of the material by analyzing the facts of the script and actions of the characters to better represent them in the editing.

Since scenes are edited out of sequence, it is also important to under stand the purpose of the scene in context of the whole story. Understanding how it informs plot and or character is critical to editorially fleshing out and not missing important elements of the scene.

V

Working Under Coverage

Once you know what story needs to be told, then you can assess the coverage to see what the director has provided to best accomplish the goals of the scene. Then establish a structure for the scene. This is important to prevent "cutting yourself into a corner."

Depending on the variables of the production schedule, budget, and skill of the director and the crew, you will have editorial choices from the coverage that could range from a wide master to close up shots of the actors. There may be over the shoulder shots or other types of tie in shots or even inserts of close action.

The director may also employ movement with the camera such as panning the camera on a left or right axis or tilting the camera up or down or any combination of tilting and panning the camera simultaneously. The camera may also move with and follow the action or be used to reveal a setting, with the use of a dolly, crane, steady cam or hand-held shot. Each type of shot or **setup** of the coverage frames, informs and focuses specifically for storytelling and character development. It's important that the editor understands how each type of shot affects the viewers visceral reaction to the story and understanding of the characters.

The director will usually shoot each setup until there is a satisfactory version or **take** to **print** that is good for camera's and actors' performances. There will probably also be multiple takes printed of some or all of the set ups.

The Dailies Grind

If editing is like having a relationship with a movie, watching dailies is the first date. It is the last time for first impressions. Since I had many awkward first dates in my youth, I know from experience. It is important while watching the dailies to be available to what the director and actors have brought with their interpretation of the material. Few in a production watch dailies as an editor should. Most in and around production will watch for interesting shots and actors' performances. An editor must view dailies in the context of how they will play when cut together. It's just as important to know what is not in the dailies as what is. This is a skill that needs to be developed, because directors and producers may inquire as to the quality of the dailies before the editor can edit the scenes. When viewing dailies, an editor needs to create a check list (if only mentally) of the coverage that is needed for the scene and what might be missing. The editor needs to confirm that each important idea, action and dialogue is covered in a setup that bests communicates it. Are the important lines of dialogue covered so that we see the speaker say the words? Are the important actions and reactions covered so that they can be communicated to the audience? These are the things to look for when watching dailies.

The better the editor understands the script, the story, and the characters, the more easily the editor can see what is working or what is missing from a scene. Since most of the important emotional transitions are not in the words but in the actions and reactions of the actors, this is where the editor needs to place extra attention when viewing dailies for what might be a problem.

On an interpersonal level, it's a good idea for the editor to give positive feedback to the director regarding dailies, along with questions or concerns. It's important that there is a sense that the director and the editor are on the same team. The editor needs to make it clear that there is an understanding of the director's intent. If there are any questions, it's important to get answers. Don't be afraid to ask questions.

When viewing dailies in preparation to cut a scene, have a copy of the script supervisor's notes for reference. First check for preferred takes, pick ups, the reason for the pick up, along with any notes that the script supervisor is passing along from the director. Make sure that each line of the scene is numbered.

Note if there are any changes in dialogue or action from the last version of the shooting script, and if it was approved by the writer or producer. Sometimes an actor will insist on changes on the set, and rather than hold up production, the changes will be allowed. Later on in post production, the producers may want the original dialogue used. This will affect the way the scene is cut. The real danger of actors changing dialogue is the unintended changing of the meaning or syntax of the scene. Improv is an interesting acting tool, but, for the most part actors are not necessarily good writers. The changes tend to make the actor more comfortable with the scene, but this may actually hurt the scene overall.

The actor's difficulty with a particular line may actually be the key to their lack of understanding of the scene.

Another actor "trick" is to attempt to change the focus of the scene from another character to them. While this is a set issue, the editor may be asked to restore the original intent. I love actors, but they are like the rest of us, with all the same short comings and insecurities

Zebras and Horses

There's an old saying, "When you hear hoof beats, think horses not zebras." When first approaching how a scene should be cut, it is wise to start with horses and move to zebras. Being drawn to the exotic or the desire to be "creative" can be tempting but usually simplicity and clarity best serves the story. Creativity must be rooted in the story and the intent of the writer and director. In a simple example, sometimes I will start a scene in a close up of a character. This works best when the idea or dialogue is more important than the setting or the physical relationship of the characters at the beginning of a scene. When I was cutting on *Picket Fences* for David Kelley, he would often use a technique of a character asking a question at the end of a scene, and the answer would be in the next scene in a close up of another character. After which the new setting was revealed in a master. It was always a fun seamless transition. Usually though, it's more important to establish the setting and the characters at the top of the scene. Most times a good director will create an opening shot to do this. As the opening shot plays, there will be a point when it no longer serves the story optimally and there is a need to cut into coverage to best tell the story.

Got It Covered ?

Below are listed some of the basic types of shots that may make up the coverage for a scene or sequence and how they affect the viewers perspective.

The clips are from a short film I directed and edited called Reflections. It stars Eunice Olsen and Anthony Montes, with Patricia Conklin. The whole movie can be seen on youtube at

http://www.youtube.com/watch?v=s4HKgK-W8GQ

The Master

is a shot in which the viewer sees the relationship of the actors to each other and the setting. A wide shot can be used to set up the scene or show movements of the characters or objects during a scene. It can be used as a relief of tension after a heated exchange between characters in close ups or even enhance tension as in a stand off between characters. It all depends on the context in which its used.

The **"tie In" and 50-50-Full Shots** are shots that narrow the focus from the master but maintain some or all of the scenes important characters or objects. It's mostly used when there is interplay between a character or characters and objects that need to be seen in the same shot

The Over the Shoulder is a shot that looks past from behind one character that features or favors another character. The **"over"** works best when it's important to feature one character while maintaining the physical relationship of both characters

Close overs or "dirty singles" are shots that maintain the relationship, while still being close

Singles and Close ups Are shots that isolate a character from other characters and most of the setting and emphasizes the expressions or emotions of that character

Inserts

are shots that are close on what a character is looking at as in a letter or picture. An insert is also a shot of an important activity that can't be seen in wider shots. For example, when a character is working on a computer and important information on the screen or the keyboard is not visible in the other coverage.

Usually, a scene will be shot starting with the master or opening shot. When using multiple cameras, there may be alternate opening shots from other cameras. If the director has not chosen a preferred shot or take, the editor needs to make a choice. Choices should be based on what the editor understands from the story and tone meetings as to the writers intent and directors vision, and what take best reveals the setting, who's there and what are they doing. Plus, which take is the most cinematically involving.

Watch how the shot plays out. Watch for the best point in the shot to make the first cut into coverage. Due to the nature of filmmaking, rarely will a scene **"play"** in the master. There may be points later in the scene where the master could be used, as for a dramatic purpose to relieve or even increase tension. It may also be used simply to show the movements of actors or reestablish the geography in the scene. Make a note, by using the page and line of dialogue from the scrip for how and where the shot will be used,

When dailies are shot with multiple cameras, it may be necessary to view them in "multi cam" mode because of the volume of material. It's important to be careful that shots or camera moves aren't missed because of splitting attention when viewing two or three set ups at the same time.

Due to time constraints during production a common multi-camera shooting technique, is for the **"B" or "C"** camera operators to shoot alternate coverage from take to take,. Sometimes these changes are not noted by the script supervisor. The editor or the assistant editor will need to note the differences from take to take.

Since digital recording is so much cheaper than film, some directors, encouraged by the assistant director to do "rolling retakes" without cutting camera, the director will have the actors go back and redo all or part of the scene. ADs like this technique, because it saves time. I'm not so sure about how most actors feel about it. The assistant editor needs to indicate where the take repeats, and possibly if there is a preferred pass.

The rest of the dailies should be viewed in the same way. Become familiar with the film. Make notes of performances and coverage of the scene using the page and line numbers from the script, as a reference.

Recovering Coverage

With the advent of HD and digital filmmaking, the ability to manipulate the material is greatly enhanced. **Blow ups and "Repos"** (short for repositions) can be made with little quality lose. Shots can be resized, reframed and moves can even be created.

Essentially, new coverage can be created in the cutting room. An over the shoulder shot can become a close up by blowing up and repositioning the shot. A two shot can become a pan from a single on one character to a single on another.

Sometimes it can be "bumpy" cutting from a moving shot into one that is static. By blowing up and panning the static shot, a move can be created to match the move on the previous cut, thus smoothing out the cut. These kinds of manipulations can be controversial depending on the sensibilities of the director and the director of photography. Therefore it's best discussed ahead of time.

Pro Choices

In each moment, the editor asks what shot and what take from the coverage will best communicate the idea or action that needs to be seen at this point in the story. There are almost infinite variations the director and DP could create with lens choice, depth of focus, camera angle and camera height or movement for shots that best serve the look and feel of the story. For example, if what is most important at a moment is to see the relationship of the characters to the setting, then a shot that is wide enough to include both would likely be the choice. If the physical relationship of two characters is important, then a shot that is closer, yet ties them together, would be preferred. If a character's reaction or emotion that is on their face is needed to be seen, a single or close up would probably be best. Coverage with a shallow depth of field also isolates the character from the environment, while greater depth of field is more inclusive. The point is to have congruity or **harmony between idea for each moment and how it's presented to the viewer.**

Size Matters, So Does Angle

The "smoothest" cuts have a size and/or angle change from the A side to the B side of the cut. The first cut into coverage is critical for setting up the cutting pattern of the scene. In traditional editing, it's desirable for the first cut into coverage to be an angle and size change to a character not favored in the master.

Below is a "Bird's eye view" illustration of a straight in cut and a reverse. The triangles represent the camera set ups with the lines showing the direction and scope being shot. The master shot and straight in closer shot on the lower right both favor "him" the camera in the upper right is a reverse that favors "Her

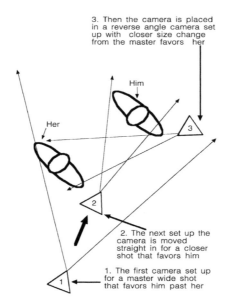

3. Then the camera is placed in a reverse angle camera set up with closer size change from the master favors her

Him

Her

2. The next set up the camera is moved straight in for a closer shot that favors him

1. The first camera set up for a master wide shot that favors him past her

For example, a character in a scene walks into a master shot set up #1 that favors him, so we see **his** face. He stops and asks a question of another character who is "not favored" so we don't see **her** face. As soon as he has finished asking his question, the first cut would be to a shot that favors her in a **reverse angle** (set up #3) that is nearly 180 degrees from the axis of the master shot.

A cut that is a **straight in** , is one that is on the same axis as the cut before it, only closer. As in the previous illustration cutting from (set up #1) straight to (set up #2) These types of cuts will magnify any mismatches and can be "bumpy" because the point of focus doesn't change from one cut to the next. The greater the size change, such as cutting from a wide master to a close up, the more likely the "**straight in**" cut will technically work. Also movement at the head of the B side may help the cut work better. Straight in cuts can be affective for emphasis for an idea or reaction.

A **straight out** cut, is cutting from a close shot to a wider shot on the same axis. The actors matching and timing become more of an issue with a cut on the same axis but slightly less with the straight out cut. When a cut has an angle change the you're directing the viewer to a new character or object and matching becomes less of an issue.

In the situation where **multiple cameras** are used and shooting wide and close in the same direction, a mismatch is less of an issue, unless there is a need to change the timing of the actor's performance which could eliminate the matching advantage of multi-cam".

The guiding rule should always be to cut to what is most important to tell the story, and then make the cut work as well as possible.

Getting Boards

The use of **storyboards** by directors in television has increased over the years. Storyboards are sketches that depict the characters and action of a scene in the intended set ups. With the demand for more complexity in production, a visual reference for the director and crew can help the production run more smoothly. The editor should also receive a copy of the storyboards. Many times referring to the storyboards can help resolve any ambiguity with the director's intent.

VI

Critical Conditioning

Previously discussed techniques for choosing what shot to be in, not only informs the editor when first putting a sequence together, it is also helpful when reviewing and critiquing sequences. If a scene or part of a scene is not working, by asking if the cut or cuts are effectively communicating the ideas of the story, will help the editor diagnose what the problem might. The key is to remain objective and not rationalize problems away. Try to view the sequence as if it is the first time you have seen it.

'Matching is for Pussies'

Excuse the un-PC phrase, but that's what was said when an editor would explain a bad cut by saying "I cut it that way because of a mismatch." One of the most frequent causes for a scene not being cut optimally, is that of a mismatching action or timing issue that the editor encounters and then tries to **"cut around"** and makes editing choices that get away from tell the story. This can have a negative impact on the cutting pattern for the rest the scene. Once the editing is going in the wrong direction, it's sometimes hard to get it back on track. Remember editing is not about matching. The reality is there are few perfect matches. If someone spots a mismatch that went unnoticed though several viewings, remind them the audience will see the movie only once.

More importantly, a cut works for the audience because what they are experiencing feels right in terms of storytelling. Minor mismatches on the cut, especially if not at or around the **point of focus** in the frame, will usually go unnoticed. The use of wider screen formats, even in television, works to the editor's advantage when dealing with minor mismatches. When trying to determine if there may be a matching problem with a cut, find in the frame where the point of focus is at the end of the A side of a cut. The viewers eye will remain in that part of the frame at least for a few frames after the cut. Chances are if the mismatch is not in the same part of the frame, it won't be noticeable. Also, using movement at the head of the B side of the cut to pull the eye away from a possible mismatch may help to make it less noticeable.

It is critical that the editor always **be aware of the point of focus** in a frame and how the viewer's eye tracks the action throughout each shot. In closer shots, the actor's eyes will tend to hold the viewers attention. Movement of any kind will also draw the attention of the viewer.

Tracking Game

Years ago, Pepsi ran a commercial with a beautiful voluptuous bikini clad woman walking out of the surf holding a can of Diet Pepsi at her side. After not getting the results expected from the ad campaign, they did some research. By **tracking the eye movement** of the people who were the test subjects watching the commercial, they discovered nobody saw the can of Diet Pepsi the models hand. The viewers attention was on the curves and face of the beautiful woman. The creators of the commercial were so caught up on the idea that a beautiful woman would help sell their product, they lost sight of what was the point of focus of the viewer's and the point of the commercial, to sell Diet Pepsi.

They changed the campaign and used a slim, attractive less provocatively dressed woman, and she held the can closer to her face, now the point of focus, so they were able to draw more attention to the product. This example shows why the editor must learn and understand how the viewer will pick up and see the most important information in the frame.

Playing in the Old School Yard

When my father started editing, editors used scissors to cut the film. The editor would cut in the middle of the frame before the head of the cut and then cut the frame after the tail. The cuts were held together with paper clips until the assistant would hot splice the sequences together so that it could be run on the Moviola and reviewed. The editor needed to know if the cuts would work based on experience even before seeing the sequence

Once, when I was still cutting with film, I tried an experiment. I cut an entire episode using the "old school" technique. By then we were using "butt splicers" with splicing tape to hold the cuts together. I didn't use scissors. I cut the film at the frame line, but I paper clipped to hold the cuts together instead using splicing tape each cut, so I didn't see the cuts until after my assistant had spliced the sequences together. To tell the truth, he wasn't happy about this experiment.

To my surprise, the episode played well with few adjustments for matching and timing issues. The editing worked, because I was focused on storytelling, rather than being bogged down with matching. Each editing decision was made based on what I felt the audience needed to see and hear for each moment Matching was secondary, because I couldn't check matching as I cut. Ultimately, if it's a choice of a perfect match or of being in the right place at the right time, choose story over technique. As an editor, you want to master the material not be a slave to it.

I found that to cut a frame or two earlier than expected rather than waiting for a match in movement will help lead the audience and make mismatches less obvious, because the eye hasn't started to move to the new point of focus. I discovered this on *St. Elsewhere*. The series was shot with very few close ups. It was shot hand held much of the time, with lots of over the shoulder and tie-in shots. This way of shooting will usually create matching issues because there are multiple characters in the frame. Expecting one actor to match from take to take is one thing. The matching issue multiplies by the number of actors in the frame. Because the producers also demanded good pace, waiting for a perfect match was unacceptable. By cutting away before the point of interest changes on the "A" side, to the beginning of new movement, action or idea on the "B" side matching is less of an issue. However, be careful with comedic situations to not cut away too soon and spoil the joke or when the statement of a character is important. Cutting away from an important line may diminish its impact.

VII

Pace Maker

In the most literal sense, it is important to always **entertain** the audience or **hold its attention.** Editing **style** is affected by each editor's tastes, sensibilities, and experience.

The most visceral aspect of style is **Pace,** or the internal rate and speed of the action and **rhythm**, the flow of the scene of the editing. Pace and rhythm have an accumulative effect on the audience. If the pace is inappropriately slow, the viewer may lose attention because of the lack of timely new information to the story. The other side of the coin, there can be confusion caused by information coming at the audience too quickly to grasp the ideas. If the rhythm is off and the editing "out of sync" the action or intent it will also negatively affect the audience's engagement in the story.

The appropriate pace is determined by presenting to the viewer **only what is needed to completely tell the story**. If more is shown than necessary, a false importance may be inferred by the audience. When information or beats are included that are not necessary or if too little is shown, the viewer is cheated of a complete understanding of the idea or action that is needed to continue to communicate the story. At a minimum, all the situations, actions described in the script, all the dialogue and story driven character development should be included in the editor's First Cut. After that, the editor should show the audience "**only what is most important for each moment to convey each idea of the story.**" This will prevent unnecessary beats, behavior, and visuals from negatively affecting pace and interfering with the editor's goal of clearly telling the story. As in a musical composition, random dynamic changes will sound discordant. The same is true of the "composition" of the cutting pattern in editing.

Performance Artist

An actor's performance is a result of talent, experience and preparation. It is also influenced by the directions given by the director. The actor's performance can be different in tone and execution from take to take. In finding the best performance, the director may give guidance in choosing the preferred set up and take. The editor should be prepared to select performance by understanding the writer's intent.

Sometimes the best performance may not be in the angle or the size shot the editor prefers. At that point, a judgment call must be made on the **trade off** between the **"best shot"** versus the **"best performance."** It's probably best to go with the best performance. However, because of the advances in digital HD video, sometimes the shot might be able to be adjusted by resizing, as by blowing up an "over the shoulder" to create a single or close up to make the preferred shot and the actor's performance coincide.

It may also be possible to take preferred dialogue from one take and sync it with the preferred picture in another take to make the shot and performance match. A little finessing of the line to sync it to the new picture will probably be necessary. A trick I learned in my days of syncing film with mag sound tracks when there was no clapper in the picture frame or on the sound: you can find sync points in the Bs, Ms and Ps of the dialogue when matched with the actors lips on the picture. Long vowels as in As, Os and Us may be shortened or even stretched by repeating sound frames to sync with the picture. Caution: too much adjusting will affect the performance and may defeat the purpose of using the line of dialogue.

Judge Not

Sometimes, you might feel an actor's performance is

substandard and there may be a wish to cut around the performance and favor other actors in the scene. This kind of editing can throw off the ideal cutting pattern. The scene could "mismatch" the intent of the scene. Another thing to remember is that once the performance is cut into the scene in the appropriate cutting pattern, the performance may work just fine. In the editor's First Cut, cutting around an actor should be avoided unless discussed with or requested by the director.

And Moving On

So much of editing is working with movement that including all an actor's movements and behavior in a cut can be seductive. However, only those movements and unspoken ideas that are needed for the story should be included. You want to eliminate any actor movements or ideas that don't contribute to the story or character development. The accumulative affect of including unnecessary parts of the actor's performance will negatively affect the overall pace and clarity of the storytelling.

VIII

The Music of Sound

In spite of what my grandfather Frank Heath said, sound is here to stay. Frank was an assistant director when sound was first being used in movies. He hated it, because it slowed down production. He was convinced it was just a fad. I think it was probably just wishful thinking at the time, because all the sounds of a movie have become such an important aspect of moviemaking.

Sometimes an actor may have trouble with the dialogue, creating unnecessary pauses or changes in the dialogue. Even a prepared actor can make acting choices that add beats, unspoken ideas or activity that may serve the acting process but do not advance the story. An actor's pauses before dialogue that are not unspoken ideas or action that advances story, character or relationship should be trimmed out.

An actor's unnecessary pauses within a line or speech can also be a problem for the editor, because they may create the need to cut away from the speaker to "pull up" the pauses in the dialogue. This can create a conflict between the need for the audience to see a character say important lines with the need for appropriate pace. I wish some actors would understand how much their performance is less than optimal when they aren't prepared, even in the hands of a good editor.

Let' Talk

Be mindful when cutting picture with dialogue and when deciding what dialogue is played with the sync picture **seen and heard** or what dialogue is **overlapped** on to other characters or visuals other than the speaker.

All dialogue is not created equal. Dialogue that is important for any story element or character development should be played in the coverage of the speaker. This is important because, by splitting the focus of the viewer between the **stronger influence of the visual over the auditory,** the importance of the spoken information is diminished by the more powerful visual.

In comedic situations it is especially critical. Playing too much dialogue or important dialogue off camera is similar to someone botching a joke by forgetting part of it or messing up the order of the set up. The punch line will fall flat and the joke teller will look foolish.

Important information for the story, character, **or joke** should be **seen and heard** for the greatest impact and understanding.

Let's Face It

When cutting to an actor to see the beginning of a line of dialogue, notice how the face starts to change just as the actor starts to speak. Often there is an unspoken idea that precedes the spoken one. Cutting just a frame or two before the actor's face changes will feel smoother and more complete than cutting when their mouth is open and in the middle of the expression change.

Under and Overheard

When deciding what dialogue can or should be overlapped, there are several things to consider. First, is there a compelling reason not to be on the speaker? Is the action of the other actor more important than seeing the speaker? Or is there a technical reason not to be on the speaker? When deciding what to overlap, the dialogue needs to be evaluated for which parts are most important for storytelling.

Many times there are parts of the dialogue that "sets up" before the main or most important idea. These can be less important and sometimes may be overlapped. There are also parts of dialogue that reinforce after the most important idea. These "supportive" parts of dialogue that come after the important idea can more likely be overlapped on another characters or action. This is effective when cutting for a reaction, if appropriate on the listening character before the speaker finishes. The important thing to remember is, most of the time, you will want to be on the speaker for the most important spoken ideas.

Dialogue Coaching

When it's important to pace up a scene and run together or "butt up" the dialogue from one character's line to the next, the last part of the line from the A side character can be overlapped slightly over the cut on to the B side picture so as to capture the beginning of the other character's change of expression.

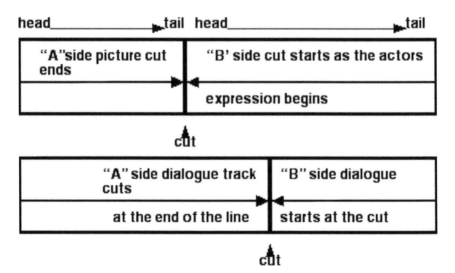

Soft sounds, such as Ss in words, smoothly cross over a cut when overlapping dialogue. Hard sounds such as Ts, Bs, and Ps will sound harsh on a cut. Therefore, place them ahead or after the cut.

If the sound and picture are cut at the same time with a straight across cut, the background sound change with the picture may make the cut "bump," especially if the background sound varies from set up to set up. Ideally, carry the "A" side sound track through the cut, up to the beginning of the first dialogue or specific sound on the "B" of the cut. This will help hide any background change from track to track.

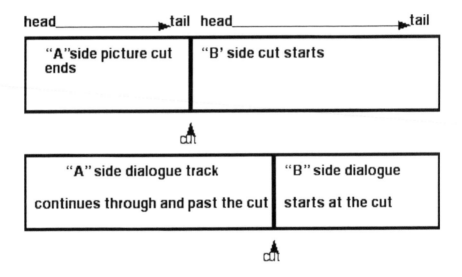

Another technique is to **"A/B"** the dialogue. By alternating the dialogue between two tracks, the background sounds before and after each line can be extended and faded up and down if needed. These techniques are more likely to be used for exterior scenes where there is less control over the background sounds.

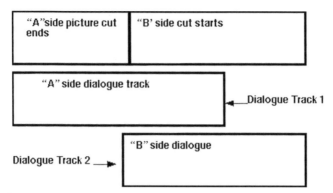

The A/B technique is also good for cutting interruptions as when one character cuts off another with their dialogue

Off camera dialogue can be edited with greater pace than on camera dialogue, but be careful not to cut it together too tightly. Off camera dialogue that is not continuous from the A side and crosses over the cut should not start too close to the head of the cut. You don't want a picture and sound change at the same time, so a little "air" is needed on the B side near the top of the cut before starting a new line. How many frames of "air" would be determined by the established pace of the dialogue in that section of the sequence. It may be helpful to listen to the dialogue without looking at the picture to tell if it sounds natural and not too rushed. I know editors who playback cut scenes this way, or they might also watch the scene without sound to get a sense of how it's playing visually.

The quality of the sound and the dialogue has a profound affect on the audience. Low, muddy, or heavy background noise will force the viewer to strain to follow the dialogue and story. The editor should only use dialogue that is on mic whether the actors share the frame or not. Sometimes because of the set up, the actors may not be ideally miced. Off mic dialogue will have more back ground noise when its level is raised and the quality of the sound will change from cut to cut. It can pull the viewer out. So you will need to use sound from another set up. This may mean syncing dialogue from takes with better sound, such as a close up.

Dialogue should be **bright** in sound quality with adequate separation from any background sounds and music which the editor is adding to the cut.

The Effects of Sound

Adding sync sound effects such as gun shots or door knocks, and background sounds, such as traffic or office **walla** will add life and dimension to a cut. These are expected when presenting an Editor's cut. How important the environmental sounds are to the scene should dictate the density and volume of the background sounds. Again, it's important not to interfere with the dialogue.

EQ (equalization sound processing) which controls the quality of the sound by manipulating the different ranges of the sound from low to high frequencies. Along with **reverb** and volume, can be used to treat the sound tracks. Adding mid range EQ processing to a track will make a sound more present and easier to hear. This is a technique to use on dialogue when it is "fighting" other sound tracks for audio dominance. The reverse is true when a background track is interfering with dialogue. Lowering the mid range EQ of the background will lower harsher aspects of those tracks . Reverb will "defocus sound" and make it less prominent even if the volume is relatively high. It may be a good choice to add reverb to music or backgrounds when asked to raise the level that may **"crowd the dialogue"** when played louder. Experiment with these tools and learn to use them to enhance your cut. The dialogue should be clear and understandable for an older middle aged man. Since they have the worst hearing of any group, they are the minimum standard. I worked with a dialogue mixer who loved to add reverb to dialogue to match the room of the scene. The problem was that the "realistic" quality of the dialogue made it harder to understand. I had to direct him to "dry it out". "Dry" refers to little or no reverb and "wet" means adding it.

When mixing the sound on your cut or supervising a final mix,"reality means nothing". Always mix with the purpose of what best tells the story and serves the situation in each sequence. Music and background sounds need to be established then "weaved" around the dialogue. As when a scene takes place in a crowded restaurant. Playing the background sounds of the workers and the people at the other tables realistically would overpower the dialogue of the principle actors. Establish the secondary sounds then lower them as the scene becomes more focused on the principles. As far as sound effects, use the sound that works best to sell the moment or situation. Even if the someone says "that's the real sound," if it sounds silly or fights the goal of the moment, find an alternative sound. Use and trust your instincts

Cue The Music

A rerecording sound mixer friend of mine sometimes refers to music as "Bondo." Bondo is the auto body repair putty that is used to smooth out the bumpy spots and fill in the voids on car doors and fenders. This kind of use of music should be last resort. A scene should be edited so the drama works without music. I usually finish editing the episode then add music, starting at the top of the show then working my way through the episode. Music should add to, but not carry the emotion or drama. In most dramatic situations, music should be in a supporting role. If the scene isn't working without music, it really won't work with it. The proper placement of music in drama is driven or triggered by the key moment of a scene, as when a character has a realization or emotional reaction to another character or a situation. Music before this point could "tip the audience off" and undermine the drama.

Unnecessary music can diminish the impact when music is needed at more dramatically critical moments. When in doubt, less or smaller is better than over the top. That being said, recent trends are for more music but more atmospheric, less "commenting" on the drama or comedy.

Music may also set a tone for a sequence as it begins to inform the audience. Action, chase or suspense scenes can be music-driven. Since there is usually little or no dialogue, the music becomes the voice of the scene. Watch such scenes without music and there is much less impact. Horror or suspense will be flat or even silly without music helping to inform the viewer of the eminent danger.

When selecting temp music for the cut, one key is to pick music that is appropriate in scale and tone to the scene and the format of presentation. For instance, music from a feature film may be out of proportion for television. Music is also an area where a director might want input or have opinions. Discussions in preproduction on the type or tone of the music could eliminate unhappy surprises in the Editor's cut.

Most times the editor will use music in a scene that is not original. In a series, music from previous episodes or sound tracks from movies of similar tone will be "temped in" to create a score. The music will rarely "drop in" and will need to be either lengthened or shortened to fit and hit the emotional and action beats of the sequence. Music repeats in tone and rhythm. By finding these musical changes and beats, music can be shortened by cutting out the music between. Sometimes the music can be lengthen, as long as the repeated sections and phrases are not too close together or too distinctive. In action or suspense sound effect booms and hits sometimes can be added for emphasis and impact. Even if you are musically trained, experimentation and experience are needed. I have been known to hide a bad music edit under a more dominating sound effect or dialogue. Then there is the old adage " If you can't solve it, dissolve it." It may be crude but can be effective.

IX

For Every Action ...

A reaction is usually an unspoken idea expressed by an actor that reveals feelings or an opinion to something said or done. When something is said or done that is provocative, cutting to the reaction of the other character or characters in the sequence is usually required. This is also true for an event in the story that would cause a character's reaction.

It's best to cut to the reaction as soon as possible after the dialogue or action that motivates it is completed. Similarly, when a character asks a question, immediately cut to the character or characters who were asked.

Conversely, you don't want to cut away from important action or a speaker's important dialogue too soon and miss the full meaning or impact. This is especially true with comedy. **Never** cut away from a funny line or action until it is completed. In comedy, there is usually a need for a reaction to a joke to maximize the humor of the situation.

Be aware that sometimes actors will anticipate a line and react too early. They are not reacting "in the moment" or as if they are hearing the line for the first time. Don't get locked into the actor's timing if it undermines the storytelling.

If the coverage allows, retime the performance and delay the reaction. When the actors share the frame, as with an over the shoulder shot, a slight mismatch usually will not be noticed if the cut is close to the action or movement of the speaker. If the mismatch is pronounced, you may be able to retime the action with the use a of split screen effect by shifting the timing of the actors if they don't overlap in the frame

The Eyes Have It

In our everyday relationships, we relate to others through their eyes as much as through what is said. No matter what is being said, the inner and emotional truth, will likely be seen in a person's eyes. That is why an actor's eyes and what is revealed about the character can be so important to the editing process.

Often before they say the dialogue, an actor will have an unspoken idea that shows or begins in the eyes. It may be important to catch this in the editing. To capture this, find the frame where the eyes start to change as the idea is being expressed and back up a frame or two to find the beginning of the cut.

The audience needs a frame or two to adjust to the new cut. When deciding the most appropriate shot to use from the coverage, the more internal the performance of the actor, the more important it is to select a shot that is close enough to the face and eyes to pick up the ideas.

Now Look

The eyes can also dictate and direct the next cut. When a character directs their look and focuses on something or someone off screen, it is likely the editor will need to cut to the character,s **"point of view" or POV.** The cut to the POV should be after the frame where the eyes lock on what is being seen.

POV Illustration

As the character looks off and as her focus locks on

cut to the character's POV

The amount and quality of eye contact between actors will inform the relationship. **An actor's eyes will focus on the character or thing on which their idea or emotion is intended.** When an actor's eyes "defocus," they may be thinking about the situation in the scene. They may also be thinking about an idea, thing or character that is not present in the scene.

Body Language

Starting with the eyes then moving out to the rest of the body, almost as much communication is done through "body language" as the words being said. These are the movements of the body that reveal the underlying reactions and emotions to a situation. You should be fluent in reading and understanding these physical expressions. Be aware whether the body language reinforces or contradicts what is being said. Tension will usually show up in the arms and hands as with the arms folded to close off. When someone is relaxed, so are the arms. Body position may also reveal tension or lack of it. If a person is facing with an open body, it can be assumed there is a lack of tension. A closed, turned away body would indicate tension or anger in the relationship of the characters. You should know how the body language helps tell the story and how it affects your choices for the best shot.

X

When Looks Could Kill

When viewing a motion picture, there is the perception of depth. Depth is perceived through the understood rules of how the brain interprets what the eyes see, such as relative size of familiar objects and converging parallel lines. We understand the proximity of the characters to the setting, objects and other characters through these rules. In reality though, motion pictures are two dimensional. Even 3D is a more enhanced two dimensional medium.

When editing motion pictures **it's all about screen direction**, for maintaining clarity and consistency of the spacial relationship between characters, their movements and the objects around them from cut to cut.

Longitude and Latitude

As far as the **"geography"** of actors or objects in a scene, in reality, it's in a flat plane. When an actor or object moves in a frame, it is in degrees of either up and down or right or left. It's like a map on the wall. When a relationship between objects or actors is established, it is in terms of right and left or up and down. That relationship should **change only during a shot, not on a cut.**

If actor "**A**" is looking left toward actor "**B**" who is looking right in a cut, the direction of those looks should continue on the next cut to a different shot. If there is action that is moving right to left through a frame on the A side of a cut . Then on the B side, at the beginning of the next cut, it should continue moving right to left. Why is this important? It's part of the "grammar" of editing. When maintaining the proper looks between characters on a cut, it maintains the uninterrupted relationship of the characters. When the looks change on a cut, it interrupts the relationship and may confuse the audience, even if subliminally.

In this wide shot the actor (Anthony Montes) playing the prisoner is on the left side of the frame and his "look" is right to the actress (Eunice Olsen) on the right and her "look" is left

For example, when cutting between close ups of two characters in a scene, if both actors are looking left, it appears they are looking at something out of frame rather than at each other. The audience may eventually figure out the intended relationship, but important ideas may be missed in the process.

In the coverage the "looks" need to be maintained.

Look---------------------------->   <----------------------------Look

He looks at her matching the established direction of the master shot

If not, confusion is created as with the shots below

Look ------------------------>   Look------------------------>

The actors are not looking at each other but looking in the same direction, and she appears to change her position in the scene from the right side over to the left. This situation occurs when the camera is placed without regard to the rules of screen direction on the set. Sometimes this can be fixed by flopping the shot. Audiences are sensitive to actors' facial features so reversing them or "flopping the shot." may not always work

XI
Jump In

Normally, a "jump cut" is a bad thing. A jump cut happens when the action of a character jumps ahead and unnaturally changes because material in the shot has been removed. However there are times when watching a character who is doing a time consuming task would be boring. It helps if the director has shot enough coverage, but even if not sometimes the action can be jumped. It works best if there is variety in the shots and each cut has a specific action that advances the progression in the task. An example would be when a character is searching a room for a lost item. By distilling the cuts down to the specific actions such as opening drawers, pulling blankets off a bed, opening the closet door and so on, a task that would take twenty minutes could be cut down to a thirty-second "montage." The key is to keep it to just the important movements and information.

Action Hero

If you're cutting an **"action sequence"** as in a fight or chase. The **logical progression of the action is important.** However, the **pace and energy** of the sequence is also critical. In many ways action sequences should be approached in the same way as any sequence, since **it's still storytelling** that is guided by the script. In fact, because there is usually less dialogue or exposition to inform the story, there is even more responsibility for clarity.

When cutting motion or action, there are two ways to approach a cut. The first is to cut **"on the action."** In this I mean, start the action or motion on the A side of the cut and complete it on the B side of the cut. Generally, it's best to cut as early as possible in the motion for a smooth and transparent transition. Again, **cutting early as possible in order to "lead the**

audience." Example: a head turn or movement with the arm that starts on the "A" side of the cut and is completed on the "B" side.

Sometimes when using movement to cut on the action, the action from each side of the cut may be different and still work and feel like continuous action to the audience. The first time I discovered this was early on in my career. In the scene, there were two actors both covered only with over-the-shoulder shots. One character, wearing glasses was smoking a pipe in his coverage. He took the pipe out of his mouth at the point where I wanted to cut. On the reverse, at the same point in the dialogue, he had no pipe in his mouth but he did remove his glasses. I cut from the A side of the cut early in the motion just as he started to take the pipe out of his mouth. Then I cut on the B side just as his glasses started to come off. The motion carried the cut. I bet my assistant that the director and the producers would never see the mismatch. They never did. Many times mismatched action can be "cheated" in this way to create the sense of continuous action.

One of the first cutting techniques I was taught by my father was to use the blur in motion to create a smooth cut. Because motion pictures are 24 still frames per second, depending on the speed of a movement some frames will have a blur in the action. The technique he taught me was to cut from the first blur from the A side of the cut to the first blur on the B side. Or "**cut blur to blur.**" Since the blur will usually happen close to the beginning of the movement, as in a fight sequence when a punch is thrown, the violent action is faster than the shutter speed of the camera, so the image blurs. This technique usually provides a smooth, transparent transition.

Sometimes waiting for the motion to start on the A side of a cut could create a stall. Instead of waiting for the movement or an action to "carry the cut," it may be better to trim any stall from the tail of the A side of the cut. Then cut to see the beginning of the motion at the top of the B side of a cut or **"cut to the action."** To make this work, find the first frame of the motion, then back up a frame or two to find the first frame of the cut. I like this technique because the editor is leading the story and not following.

One way to energize a sequence is to trim the action to a minimum using the movement to **"cheat the action."** This is called **"under matching."** Using a minimum of action starting on the tail or the "A side" of a cut, cut to as late as possible into the action at the head of the "B" side of the cut. The only requirement is that you still comprehend the idea and intention of the action.

In a fist fight, does the audience need to see the "wind up" of the punch or can it be trimmed straight to the punch going forward to impact? As the fight scene progresses, the action can be trimmed closer to the important moments as the scene reaches its climax.

On the first pass in cutting the sequence, it's probably best to cut with all the action as it naturally plays. Later, trim up the sequence where it can be trimmed. This process may take several passes.

Sometimes there is an action or an event, like an explosion or a collision, that for maximum impact, may play best if the speed of the action is changed to slow motion. In the beginnings of filmmaking the camera operator would hand crank the camera. For slo-mo the operator would crank faster, or "over crank" to create more frames per second when projected. The term "over-cranked" is still used today when something is shot for slo-mo. If the action is not shot for slo-mo and needs to be slowed down, a motion visual effect may be used to slow the action down. This may not always the best technique because it's essentially repeating frames and may not look as fluid had it been shot in 48 or 72 frames per second. This technique in film is referred to as "over cranking" from the original hand crank cameras used in silent filmmaking. Conversely, the technique called "under cranking" will record fewer than 24 frames per second and will speed up the action when played. This was used to great comedic effect in the movie *The Gods must be Crazy* and was also often used on the television show *Gilliagin's Island.* BTW, silent movies were shot at 18 frames per second, and now most of the time they are played back at 24 frames per second. The jerkiness of these movies is caused by this.

Another technique to better experience the action is to repeat some of the action from the A side of a cut to the B side. As with, some or all of the fireball from an explosion repeating as it ascends into the sky is always . I call this "**over matching**" This technique will underline or emphasize the action and give it a more dramatic presentation.

Cutting (before the) Edge

There are many situations when an object's or a character's movement is continuous from the A side of a cut to the B side in the next shot. Like a pitcher throwing a baseball on the A side of a cut to the catcher catching the ball on the B side. Rarely is it necessary for an object or person to completely exit the frame on the "A" side. Most times the A side can be trimmed well before the object or character exits frame. It's important to allow for just enough movement to indicate the direction of the movement. Then, when cutting to the B side, pick up the object or character just a frame or two before it enters the frame. Since most "Stalls," or unneccesary delays happen at the end of a cut, this technique helps pace up the action.

In fact, if for any reason, such as miss timing of action or matching problems, when there is a need to add "extra frames" to a cut, it is usually best to put the extra frames on the head of B side of the cut. Since there will be **new information for the audience, it will be less likely to feel like a stall** in the action.

Here and There and ...

"Parallel Action" is the intercutting of action from different settings it is usually done because the action will eventually converge. An example of this would be the classic scene from so many Western movies where the settlers are under attack from the "local tribe" and are hoping the calvary arrives in time to save them. By cutting back and forth between the Calvary racing to the scene of the skirmish as things get more and more desperate for the settlers, there is a ratcheting up of the tension. This is especially true when it looks like the Calvary might not make it in time. Once the pattern of intercutting is established the cuts should get shorter as the action gets closer to its convergence

Parallel Action can also be used to thematically contrast actions or story lines. The contrasting of the Baptism scene with the "settling of the family business" in *The Godfather* is one of the most famous examples.

There are scenes scripted consecutively that may have issues with pace. Sometimes they may be able to be broken up and intercut using parallel action techniques to pace up the story by trimming out unnecessary actions. Thus "pacing up" both scenes.

Stand and Sit-uation

Standing and sitting are such a natural part of behavior they can often be a part of a scene's blocking. It may be a good opportunity to cut into coverage from a wider shot. A mistake I often see is when an editor will cut to an "empty frame" to see a character enter and then sit into the shot. Cutting to a shot that doesn't include the character's face is uninteresting and makes the viewer aware of the editing. A more fluid approach is to cut from the A side of the wide shot as the character is in the act of sitting. The end of the cut should be the first frame his butt hits the seat. Then on the B side repeat one frame of the action of his butt hitting the seat to complete the act of sitting. This will be a transparent cut and the audience will never lose track of the character's face.

When a character is rising out of a seat, just reverse the previous technique and cut early in the characters movement to rise out of the seat into the next shot .

A similar technique can be used when cutting walking or running. Cut just as the character's foot hits the ground on the A side of a cut. Then, on the B side, repeat one frame of the action. This will make for a transparent transition. What is interesting is that matching which foot doesn't seem to matter, the audience understands the cut as continuous action.

When these techniques are used, the speed of the motion may affect the overlapping of the action on the cut. Slower motion would need less overlapping and quicker motion would need more overlapping of action

XII

Vandals Sack Rome

There is an old production joke. The script's description of a scene is "Vandals sack Rome." Since production schedules are based on page count, the production manager says to the director "It's just an eighth of a page, you should be able to shoot it in a morning." It's funny, but what happens to the editor who gets a mountain of film with very little direction or guidance from the script or director? Editors are storytellers, so from what is known from the script, and after viewing the dailies, a narrative should be created. Again, by asking the 5 W questions, conclusions can be made about what needs to happen and what is the point of the scene. The editor can then write a "script" for the scene as a guide. A battle, while chaotic for the participants, is a "scene." It should be part of the motion picture that advances the story for the audience.

In Transition

A transition is a passage in the story that moves from one setting or time to another. Except for the beginning of the movie, there will always be a scene, setting or sequence preceding the beginning of each sequence. It may be to a new idea, as to a new location or story line with different characters. It may be the continuation of story and characters from the preceding scene with a passage of time. It can go from question to answer. At the end there may be a completion of the scene or there may be an idea or action that sets up the story segueing to the next sequence. The end of the last cut of a scene sets up the next scene. What is important is that the transition is an effective connection that holds the audience's attention and interest.

Wipes and **flips** are technical transitions that are used mostly when a cinematic transition was not planned for or shot. Except for a few situations, they are mechanical and inorganic to the material. Some exceptions might be if the picture is stylized with specific visual effect transitions in mind as with a sci fi, period, or fantasy story. Another use would be when the scene is changed during editing and the original transition is trimmed or lifted and then a manufactured transition may be needed. Producer Harve Bennett once told me "you can flip from anywhere to anywhere." Perhaps just a slight exaggeration. What these types of transitions do though is tell the audience that we're changing the time, the location or both of the story

Dissolving, which is overlapping a fade out from one scene and fading up to the next, usually tells the audience there has been a passage of time. Because the shots will be visually overlapping throughout the dissolve, it's important that enough material is shot to cover the length of the **dissolve.** For example, in the outgoing scene the actors end their dialogue and the camera pans with them as they walk off and we want to start a dissolve that lasts three seconds and at the end of the dissolve, in the incoming scene, we want the actors to start talking. We need at least three seconds of incoming pan or action before the dialogue starts because of the overlapping action. Again too much is better than not enough.

In television, **fade ins** and **fade outs** are used to begin and end acts and give separation from the commercials. Fades in a movie will give a strong sense of passage of time. In television, they are rarely used within the story because they bring a complete halt to the action.

Because many interior scenes are shot on a **sound stage,** sometimes there will be no exterior shot to establish the location for a transition into the scene. Ideally, **the editor and director can work together to research and chose a shot of an exterior of the scene** for the **production designer** to match the style of the exterior to the style of the interior for the design and construction of the **set**.

Finding an establishing shot for the scene after it has been shot from a **stock library** is less than ideal but may be necessary. Stock libraries, found on the internet, can also be a resource for establishing cities or locations with iconic shots that let the audience know where the story is taking place. While there is a cost to these shots, the advantage is production value without the much greater cost to production . The disadvantage is that they may not match the look and feel of the rest of the production if selected after **principal photography**.

There are locations that most audiences recognize easily. Manhattan from across the river with the Brooklyn Bridge in the foreground needs no further explanation as to the location of the story. The same is true with Paris and the Eiffel Tower or the Colosseum in Rome.

Another way to inform the audience where the setting is may be to put a title with the name of the city or location superimposed over the establishing shot. Creative use of music and sound evocative of the setting can also enhance the transition to a new location.

XIII

Judge Not

After the first cut, the editor's job changes to that of realizing the ideas of the director and then later the producers and writers. As an editor you needs to be careful of judgment, on how the director has decided to shoot the movie. You need to be available if the dailies are not as pre visualized and avoid becoming critical. It's important to get onboard. The editor and director need to be a team.

That Being Said

I was involved in a pilot as a producer. The director told the editors that he wanted to be "surprised." He encouraged them with "don't give me the expected." One of the editors took this to heart and really "thought outside the box" and cut a scene very unusually in sound and visual effects. He sent it to the director for his thoughts. I was instructed to fire the editor the next day. A cautionary tale.

Pulling in the Same Direction

I know a director who, when he walks the sets and location, tries to "see the movie." No matter how much communication there has been in prep between the director and editor, there is a possibility that the editor didn't "see the same movie" and the director will be disappointed with the editor's first cut. The editor needs to not take it personally. It's just as likely that the director will be pleasantly surprised that the cut is playing better than expected. Many times it's just seeing the unexpected that will throw a director in the first viewing of a cut. What's most important is that the director is secure that the editor is there to realize the director's vision. The editor should reassure the director that that is the case.

When you get comments on the cut, you will quickly learn if the director has the vocabulary and skills to give clear and specific editing notes. If not, then you'll need to use your best powers of interpretation to understand what about the cut the director wants to change.

I once got an editing note from a director, "This scene is asymmetrical." I viewed the scene with the note in mind. I remembered having problems with one of the actors performance when first putting the scene together. I had "cut around" what I perceived as the weaknesses in the acting. In the editing I had favored the other actor more in the scene instead of what the storytelling would have called for. After the note, I adjusted the cuts to put the scene back in balance. This is an example of trying to make a fix, where the solution is worse than the problem.

These kinds of issues are where the editing can get away from being at its best. It can be a mismatch that forces the editor away from the preferred editing point or an unwanted pause in the actor's performance that gets covered with an unmotivated **cut away.** If an editor is not skillful, these "solutions" can be awkward and bump for the director and trying to explain the reason for a bad cut, won't make it better. The editor needs to find a better solution.

"The scene is cutty."

When an editor gets the note that the scene is "cutty," it's usually that the editor has cut more than is necessary to tell the story. Cutting to unnecessary reactions or cutting away from the character speaking to the listener unnecessarily during important dialogue. Look at the cutting pattern. Are there cuts that are not necessary to the scene? Also look for cuts that are too quick or short, so that the viewer misses some of what the cut was meant to inform. Cutting away too quickly from an important line of dialogue, the viewer may feel cheated, even if on a subliminal level. Adding unnecessary cuts can diminish the impact of the more important ones and the scene can lose focus.

"The scene seems slow."

Unneeded pauses, particularly true if added after one character's dialogue, that delays the reaction of another character, can have an accumulatively negative affect on the pace of a scene.

There may be actor's "**wind ups**" to a line of dialogue that don't add to the story or character. Because actors are dynamic and motion is inherent in editing, it's easy to be drawn to adding these moments and beats. In reviewing cut scenes the editor needs to be aware of these false moments and should trim them out. A writer/producer I worked with would often say, "Let them act while they're talking."

A needed beat or pause if left out will give the viewer the feeling they have missed something. The key is, if the silent moment is a reaction or other unspoken dialogue expressed by the actor that advances the story or character development, it should be included. Pauses and beats that don't inform should be trimmed.

"Give them what they want not what they ask for."

If the director is having trouble articulating what is not working, ask questions that might help focus on the problem. What were you looking for? What were you trying to accomplish with the scene? What's missing? What's bumping for you? The editor should also take a fresh look at the scene for what might be the problem.

What the editor doesn't want to do is make a bad change because the director was unable to clearly state what is not working. Doing so, risks making the director and the editor look bad, and that could hurt their working relationship. It's important for the editor to figure out what the director means in the note not what was asked for. This is perhaps one of the trickiest aspects of the editor/director relationship. It's also a part of the craft that needs to be mastered to become a successful editor.

Sometimes, if the cuts are working technically, it can be a challenge for the editor to see what isn't working in a scene. The technique could be good and the editing smooth, but the story telling may be lacking. It's a "forest for the trees" situation. For example, in the "John and the Bob" scene used earlier. Because the John character is so dynamic, coming in and yelling at Bob, the editor could focus the editing on John. While the scene may be technically well cut, the director wants to tell the story of the Bob's reaction to John's behavior. The editor needs to be available to the director's intent for the scene.

Stay fresh

When cutting on a **Moviola** with an eight inch viewer and the time consuming task of finding trims, few directors wanted to spend any time in the cutting room. Notes were given by the director and changes viewed in a screening room. Now, with sixty inch monitors and comfortable couches, the cutting room is a more inviting place for the directors and producers. What the screening room gave was a little distance for the director from the notes session to seeing the changes.

Making Sausage

If you like to eat sausage, it's probably best you don't watch it being made. After the first pass of notes, I think it's a good idea for the director to leave the editor alone to make the changes. First, it forces the director to focus on what needs to be changed by giving notes for the whole show. Since the first set of notes will likely have the most changes, the editor will work better without the pressure of the director in the room. Sometimes an editor needs to explore options to come to the best execution of a note. This can be tedious for the director sitting in the room. Secondly, when the director watches the next pass, having not been in the cutting room to watch each change being made, there is a better chance for an objective viewing, allowing for a better judgment of how well the changes worked and how the show is playing. Once one is involved in the editing process, whether editor, director, or producer, it is difficult to stay objective when reviewing editing changes.

Take Note

The editor should discuss with the director how they can best work together during editing. Misunderstanding or missing notes can cause much frustration for both. The editor needs to be organized and ready to get notes from the director; have the show available with the running time code for reference, have a continuity with a running time code indicating the beginning of each scene, have the script supervisor's script notes available. Having the assistant editor available to take notes is ideal. The editor shouldn't move past a note until it is completely understood. Disregard any impatience with the speed of the notes process. Getting it right is much more important and will help eliminate future disappointments.

Last First Impression

The editor needs to do the best and most complete job possible on the Editor's Cut. An editor will lose credibility if the work on the Editor's Cut is sloppy or slip shod. The Editor's Cut is the last opportunity for the editor to say "This is how I think the movie should play." After that, the editor's job is to realize the visions of the director and later the producers. It's important for the editor to embrace and commit completely to all phases of the editing process.

XIV

Post Imperfect

Most of the time an editor is a "hired gun" brought in to work with material without having much control over the quality. The performances might not be up to par and the coverage may be lacking. **If you've taken the job, then commit to the job**. Without judgment, get the most out of the material that is possible.

Motion pictures evolve throughout the editing process. The editor should remain available to new and different approaches to the material and be a problem solver not an obstacle to changes. Editing is re-editing. After the editor's First Cut, the editor must **always be the audience's representative** in the cutting room. Work without any agenda other than making the best possible motion picture.

Look and Learn

The best way to learn editing is by doing editing. That is what I did as an assistant editor. The more I cut, the more I learned. With the emergence of relatively cheap digital moviemaking, the possibility of shooting and cutting one's own projects is greater than ever before.

Another way to learn is with downloaded or DVD motion pictures. With the ability to control forward, pause, slow mo and reverse, scenes can be viewed and reviewed. As an approach, pick and view a scene from a motion picture. What's the first impression? Can you answer the basic questions of who, what, when, where, and why? Was it entertaining and engaging? Re-watch the scene and note the cutting pattern. What dialogue is on camera and what is overlapped? If the scene works, make notes of the aspects of how it was cut that made it effective. Likewise, if the scene didn't work, critique it, keeping in mind what has been discussed in this book to figure out why the scene doesn't succeed. This can be used for future reference when cutting scenes with similar elements.

Below is a selection from an article I wrote for the *Editors Guild Magazine*,"*Tail Pop*" column, Sept.-Oct. 2010, on the Coen Brothers' movie *Millers Crossing* using this kind of analysis.

Miller's Crossing opens in an insert as ice drops into an Old Fashion glass and whiskey from a cut crystal decanter is poured. As the camera pulls back, we hear an Italian mob boss complaining to an Irish mob boss about the Jewish bookie Ernie selling tips on fixed fights. "It's getting to where an honest business man can't expect a fair return on a fixed fight." Without any sense of irony, he rants about the lack of ethics while his henchman Dutch stands guard. The protagonist Tom, an observer, is introduced first out of focus moving in the background. The delay in seeing his face enhances his importance. With this unconventional and creative approach to the beginning of a movie, I was involved immediately. The editing, the photography, and the dialogue had me wanting more.

For the full article
https://www.editorsguild.com/Magazine.cfm?articled=906

Final Cut

Nothing that has been discussed should be construed as a limitation on creativity. On the contrary, the techniques and observations discussed have allowed me to focus on creative choices and free me from being bogged down with technical issues. The one thing I've learned is that I never stop learning. As long as you are open and available, you will be able to learn. My hope is that I've created an approach to editing that allows the editor to bring his or her own life experience, intelligence and creativity to each project.

For Directors Only

Information and advice for directors or those who want to be a director and achieve better results and relationships in the cutting room

The Director and the Editor

The story goes, this editor was bragging to the director about how he did such a great job of "saving the picture." The director countered with "Did you cut anything I didn't shoot." In many ways this story represents the problems and pitfalls of the editor/director relationship. Why does the editor feel the need to deride the director to enhance his own contribution? Did the director fail to provide the needed material to clearly tell the story or did he fail to communicate his vision to the editor? Basically the story illustrates the natural tension between an editor and the director.

In Prep

It is the job of the director to understand the writer's story and then realize it. There are directors with a strong visual sense, while others strength is fleshing out actors performances. The best are good at both. Directors must make many decisions and choices during prep, and there is much discussion about every aspect of the production. Wardrobe, make up and camera tests are done. The director and producers work with casting, the art director, props and all the departments of the production so that hopefully everyone is clear on what picture the director intends to make. It's a big machine that needs a confident and talented person to work efficiently and communicate clearly. What is missing many times is the director prepping the editor in the same way. In an ideal world the editor would be with the director during all aspects of prep so that the editor could see what the director wants visually, tonally, and with the actors' performances. Unfortunately, many times, the editor is not a part of the team until the first day of production. In episodic television, editors work in rotations with two or three editors. During the director's prep the editors are usually completing previous episodes, which keep them too busy to participate.

Most shows have script and "Tone Meetings" where the director meets with the writer and/or show runner to discuss the script. In the script meeting, which occurs early after the script is first published, the director will usually give his feedback and suggestions. The purpose of the tone meeting, which happens closer to the start of production, is to insure that all are on the same page in regard to the look, feel, and intent of the story and the actors' performances. It is critical that the editor be a part of this meeting and should ask questions and take notes to use to clarify any issues where there is confusion about the intent of any part of the story. With technology being what it is, even when the editor is not at the same location as the writer and director, a phone or internet patch can be made to allow for his participation.

On the Set

Transitions

The director and the editor need to be in sync as to the transitions from one scene to the next. First, a character's behavior needs to be consistent with the previous scene. Take the simple transition of a scene ending with the actor opening a door and walking through it and the next scene starting as the actor comes through the other side. It's not unusual for these scenes to not be shot consecutively. The pace and attitude of the actor needs to be same from one scene to the next.

Scenes don't just end. Whatever the last frame of a scene is, in some way, it's setting up the next scene. Does the actor need to react to something said or done or should the actor move out of frame? The director needs to plan how the end of the scene plays against the beginning of the next.

A note to directors, don't say "cut" too quickly at the end of a take. The actors, camera and sound stop working on "cut". It's better to have a little too much material at the end of a scene than not enough.

The best transitions engage the viewer while moving the story along. The first question to ask is what the transition needs to accomplish. Is it a new setting or time? Does the audience need a breather because of the intense action or emotion of the last scene, or is the next scene starting with movement and action? Are we going to a different storyline or is the action continuous? These are the kinds of questions the director and editor should discuss, so they are clear on the look and feel of the important transitions.

While a good transition informs the audience of everything necessary to set up the incoming scene, there shouldn't be more than what's needed. Time is usually limited, especially in television. No matter how pretty the incoming transition is, if it's not engaging and informative, it will likely be trimmed later when the director is no longer a part of the editing process. Directors can "fall in love" with shots because of the aesthetic or even the time and effort on the set to get the shot. Every shot needs to be judged on its impact on the movie. Most television shows are plot, character, and dialogue driven. These elements need to be a part of the transition. Any part of the transition without them will likely be lost. An actor walking without purpose becomes "shoe leather," as will a pan at the top of the scene that doesn't contain the elements of the story . It will also have a negative impact on the perceived pace of the movie.

Generally, it's good to give the actors a "clean entrance" into the scene. This gives the editor more options. If the actors are in the frame at the top of the scene, it is best that they have some activity before the start of dialogue. This will help make for a smoother transition. For example; it is very clunky to cut into a scene if the actor is just starting to walk and talk when the director calls "action." A step or two before the dialogue starts will allow the editor to find a smooth transition into the scene. If not you may force the editor to start the dialogue before the beginning of the scene by "pre lapping" it over the previous scene. This may be a great transitional device, but it should be a creative choice not a "fix."

"Pick a take"

Next to the director, the busiest person on the production crew is the **script supervisor.** Monitoring the actors' dialogue and actions, tracking and logging camera setups and consulting with the director on what coverage is needed to properly edit the scene, makes the script supervisor critical to the director/editor communication and process.

While the advances in technology have increased both the number of setups and printed takes possible, it has also made the script supervisor's job tougher. Once production starts, the director indicating to the script supervisor preferred takes and any notes given for the editor concerning camera or actors performances may be the only communication the director has with the editor.

The inevitable changes and adjustments that happen during production need to be communicated to the editor. No matter what the director planned for camera, actor blocking and performance based on prep, an actor's interpretation can change the dialogue and movement of a scene. Also, changes in production or unforeseen obstacles may also force changes in the script from what was originally prepped and discussed. The director, through the script supervisor, needs to keep the editor in the loop. The script along with the script supervisor's notes are the editor's bible during the editing of the first cut.

Movement

In a play, the movement of the actors changes the focus and emphasis of the story and directs the audience's attention. However in a movie, the camera's point of view and editing directs the audience's attention, allowing the actors movement to be more organic to the story. That being said, there is a tricky balance between blocking a scene for the actor's performance and the needs of the camera. The actor's performance and movements are driven by the dialogue and descriptions in the script. "Content dictates movement" is a time tested axiom. What is true for the actors is also true for camera movement, whether **panning** or **dollying** to follow the movement of an actor or object in the scene, or moving while the actors are still. The movement needs to be germane to the scene and the storytelling. **A moving shot at the top of a scene that does not include dialogue, important action or information will be the first thing cut out no matter how pretty the shot.**

The unsteady movement with hand-held camera techniques gives an immediacy as with a news story or documentary that can create a natural tension in the scene. It also allows a good camera operator to organically follow the action. Camera movement to compensate for what the director thinks is missing from the scene usually indicates the director's inability to flesh out the scene or a lack of understanding of the material. Answering what in the scene requires the camera to move is the only way to decide how and why the camera should move. Movement is one of the most valuable colors a director has in his pallet to create a mood or give energy to a scene.It may be desirable to shoot a scene in an interesting way, but interesting shots may not always tell the story in the best way or work cohesively with the other shots of the scene. Understanding how shots interplay in the context of framing and composition is critical. For each cut of a sequence, the angle and distance of the camera to the subject helps tell the audience what is most important for each moment of the story.

In a wide master shot, the viewer sees the relationship of the actors to each other and the setting. In a close-up of an actor the director isolates and narrows the view to emphasis expression and emotion

By expanding the depth of field in coverage, the director can include the background and show, if it's important to the storytelling, how it interplays with the actors. By narrowing the depth of field, the director makes the moment more about the character. Each choice evokes something different for the viewer.

The angle of the camera is also critical to the involvement of the viewer with the characters. If the actor looks straight into the camera as in a news broadcast, the audience feels they are no longer a viewer but a participant in the story. The movie stops being about the characters in the story. Conversely, as the camera set up is moved away from the actors' faces, the viewer's involvement decreases. Once you "lose two eyes" in the shot, it becomes a profile, losing dimension and becomes disengaging.

One of the least interesting shots is a **50-50** where two actors face each other and the camera shows both in profile. It's a flat, uninteresting shot. Editorially it's an awkward angle to cut from into closer coverage.

Unless there is a compelling reason, it's better to pick an actor to **favor** in the shot or move the actors, camera, or both. Editorially, a good master shot establishes and "ties in" all the actors in the scene. The first cut into coverage sets up the cutting pattern for the scene. Plan when to cut into coverage the first time to best tell the story in the scene. Knowing this when blocking the actors or planning camera set ups and moves, the director can eliminate awkward cuts into coverage.

For example, cutting from a moving master shot into a static closer angle may be jarring. By planning to have the camera stop moving before the planned cut or adding complimentary movement to the coverage will make for a smoother cut.

Screen Direction

Screen direction issues may be a result of poor planning when blocking the camera and the actors for the scene.

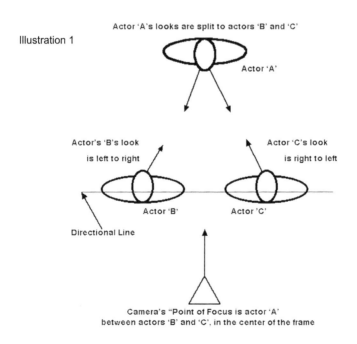

Illustration 1

Actor 'A's looks are split to actors 'B' and 'C'

Actor 'A'

Actor's 'B's look is left to right

Actor 'C's look is right to left

Actor 'B'   Actor 'C'

Directional Line

Camera's "Point of Focus is actor 'A' between actors 'B' and 'C', in the center of the frame

A common example is in a scene that has three characters where the first camera set up is placed (*Illustration 1)* between two actors who have their backs to camera and the actor in the middle, the **point of focus**, facing camera. This "splits his looks" to the other two actors. One "look" to the other actors is right to left and the other "look" is left to right. In this situation the rest of the coverage is going to be problematic. When the camera is placed on the reverse side for coverage it will cross the "Directional Line" and the actors "looks" will not match the first set-up that is established for the scene and they will change during editing. As discussed in section X, **When Looks Could Kill, "It's all about screen direction"** as in the first set up.

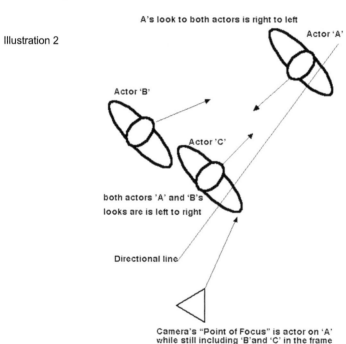

Illustration 2

A's look to both actors is right to left

Actor 'A'

Actor 'B'

Actor 'C'

both actors 'A' and 'B's looks are is left to right

Directional line

Camera's "Point of Focus" is actor on 'A' while still including 'B'and 'C' in the frame

In Illustratoin 2 set-up the camera does not cross the "Directional Line" which maintains the direction of the actors looks from one set-up to the next. The other issue with the first set-up in *Illustration 1*, is that placing the actor or any "point of focus" in the center of the frame tends to not be very interesting or visually pleasing composition.

Composition and Editing

Composition effects editing. Understanding the interplay of the composition of the coverage is essential. Using the **Rule of Thirds** as in classical composition technique is helpful when setting up shots for coverage of a scene. If a frame is divided in thirds, both vertically and horizontally, the **point of interest** or focus will usually fall where the lines intersect rather than at the center of the frame. This is also true for objects or characters that are used as framing elements in the shot. Still, composition in filmmaking is not just about interesting, informative and evocative shots, but also about how the shots work and interplay with each other during editing.

Below the actors eyes being the "point of interest" land where the top third and the left third intersect.

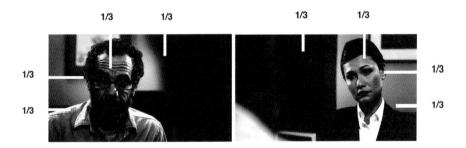

In the reverse angle below, the eyes again fall along the top third, but this time on the right third vertical line. Using the rule of thirds is helpful in creating shots that smoothly cut together, because it "weights" the shot for more room in the frame for the direction of the "look"

When we relate to people non verbally, it is mostly through their eyes, so in closer coverage the eyes will be the point of interest of the shot. If, in the Master, actor "A" is on the left side of the frame looking left to right at actor "B" in the closer shot, the eyes should be framed at the upper left part of the frame where the "rule of thirds " lines would intersect. On the reverse coverage of actor "B," the eyes would be where the lines intersect on the upper right side of the frame. The rule of thirds is helpful with all sizes and angles. Not only is this type of composition pleasing, it also makes for smoother editing by creating clarity and consistency throughout the coverage. This also "weights" the framing, allowing more room in the frame ahead of the actors look off camera. It's usually best to not to frame the actor look too close to the edge of the frame.

Another way to keep the actors "looks" engaging is to **"cheat"** them. This is done by having the off camera actors positioned close to the camera when shooting coverage. In a situation where an actor is looking off camera to more than one actor, the actual distance between the off camera actors should be cheated by compressing their positions closer together and closer to camera, so the on-camera actor's look doesn't get too far from the lens. Using multiple cameras can complicate cheating the looks. Below are illustrations on "cheating" the off camera looks

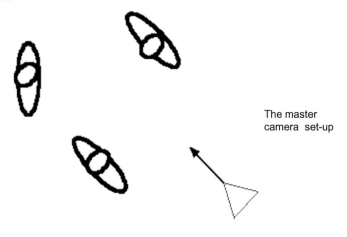

The master
camera set-up

In this previous camera is set up with the camera in the master where we see all the actors in their natural positions.

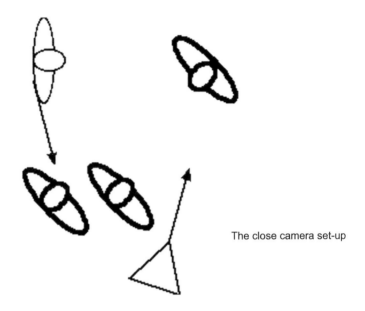

The close camera set-up

When the camera set up is moved to shoot the closer shot on the actor on the right, both the other actors positions should be "cheated" closer to the camera for better "looks" between actors.

If the actor in the middle isn't moved, as in the above illustration, the look of the actor on the right to the actor in the middle would be in profile in the coverage and thus less engaging.

Multi cam

There is an old saying in the **cutting room,** "footage is not coverage." An editor can get mountains of film in **dailies** and still not get the necessary pieces of coverage to properly edit a scene. This is the risk when shooting with multiple cameras. Most TV sitcoms are shot with four cameras before an audience. The look and feel is of a play and is very uncinematic . The more cameras that are used, the more there may be a need to compromise the quality of the angles of the coverage. The lighting also needs to be more general and flatter. If the director doesn't plan carefully, there is the risk of shooting set-ups that are less than optimal.

Attempting to shot both sides of the action at the same time forces the cameras away from the actors to avoid the cameras from photographing each other. The director of photography is also forced to light most of the set to accommodate the cameras shooting in both directions. This can become time consuming and may not work in the days schedule.

This type of look may work in a lighter more comedic scene. However when the scene is dramatic, it won't be as affective. With the cameras shooting in the same direction, they compete for the most effective angles. The director may want to shoot an **over-the-shoulder** and a **close-up** on the same actor at the same time. One of the cameras can be forced away from the desired angle to accommodate the other camera. One thingfor is sure, the close up should be set first. Because the actor's **"look"** is most critical in the closer shot, that shot should be set with the actor's eye line close to the lens.

Placing the cameras on both sides of an actor can create problems with screen direction as the other actors looks will be different with each angle. Also actors positioned in the foreground will change between angles which will then be distracting in editing Multi-cam is a tool that needs to be used smartly. While a great time-saver, the elements for effective coverage and storytelling still need to be followed.

Actors and Camera

A director I know says, "Never talk to an actor unless you have to." This is not as cynical as it sounds, and there is a lot of wisdom in it. Explaining the scene to the actors and giving a lot of direction before and during rehearsal can backfire and may be a waste of time. An actor's need for a lot of discussion of the scene before the rehearsal and blocking may indicate a lack of preparation. The actor may not have done their homework and is doing it on the set.

Have a plan for the scene but allow for the actor's input. This will make for a smoother running set. The best way to get the actor's take on a scene is for them to show you what they have brought to it.

The director should establish the actors' positions at the top of the scene. Then stand where the camera will be and let the actors run the scene. Actors will tend to play the scene, aware that you are the audience and camera. The more that's right with what they have brought in, means there is less the director needs to direct. This also informs the DP and the crew as to the director's intentions for how the scene is to be shot.

Rehearsal

Mismatches in performance and movements are the biggest obstacles to making good editorial choices. While the primary responsibility to monitor the actors movements is the script supervisor. It is a technical and inorganic solution to mismatches. If a scene is rehearsed properly and the actors are secure in their dialogue, performances and blocking, they will naturally match from one angle to the next. A few extra moments of rehearsal and discussion so that all are clear on the intent and performances before beginning to shoot will save time during shooting. Being "inspired" midway through shooting a scene, may create big problems later in the **cutting room** if the performances don't match set-ups previously shot.

Keeping the actors' blocking and movements **content driven** will make the needed adjustments for camera easier for the actors. When blocking an actor to move, be ready to give a simple reason for that move. Having the reason is good for all. Actors are "doers." The more the direction is in the form of an action that they can accomplish, with the least amount of interpretation, the better. The reality is that actors will need to adjust their positions and movements to accommodate the camera and lighting to create the most effective set ups. The more comfortable they are with the blocking, the easier these adjustments will be. Finally, if you can't articulate a reason for an actor to move, maybe there isn't a good reason. Adding movement won't replace what may be missing in content or performance in the scene.

Sound Advice

In emotional scenes there may be a tendency for actors to want to overlap the dialogue. This may create technical and creative problems later on in editorial. Unless the scene is about the characters not listening to each other and the overlapping is intentional, the audience may miss important information. It may feel good in the moment, but there is a danger in the actors anticipating the next line and reacting prematurely. The characters come off as disingenuous. Even if overlapping dialogue is the desired end result in the performance, it's impossible for actors to overlap exactly in the same way in every take and angle. Later in editing, intercutting between preferred angles can become impossible requiring the need to **ADR or loop** the dialogue later in post. When rerecording the dialogue much later on an ADR stage without the other actor to play off of, matching the performance becomes difficult.

Once, when I was producing in television, there was a very

difficult scene to shoot. One character was to sing while three other characters were yelling at him, each with their own issue. The singing was prerecorded so that we could separate the singing from the spoken dialogue in editing and then later on the mixing stage. I arrived at the set to find out the singing actor had persuaded the director to throw out the playback recording and let him sing it "live" in production. This would have been a sound nightmare with every actor in the scene coming back to rerecord dialogue and singing on a looping stage. I interceded to convince them it would be a mistake. The singing actor pulled me aside and reasoned there would be no problem because he could match his singing each time from take to take. While virtually impossible to do, I conceded the point to his great talent. I then pointed out that the other actors didn't have his ability and that they would never be able to match their performances as he would. He thought about it for moment and saw my point. We used the playback pre record and shot the scene as planned.

In comedy, overlapping is always problematic. The construction of the dialogue in comedy is critical. All the dialogue needs to be heard clearly for the humor to work. Missing a part of the dialogue is like telling a joke and leaving important information out. It ruins the humor. The same is true in drama, just less obvious. The writer worked hard and thoughtfully writing the dialogue. Shooting and recording all the dialogue as written is critical. If the actors can't or won't perform the scene without overlaps, ask for takes that are "clean" for sound editing. Remember the film is not made on the stage, it's made in editing. How the actor "feels" is of little importance to the end result but don't tell the actor that.

Ad-libs and improv are also problematic, especially if part of the scene has already been shot. With the right director and the right actors and usually in a feature where time and budget are less of an issue, they are great tools for creativity. An actor and director can find an emotional thread or truth of the scene. However more often than not, if an actor has trouble with a line, there is usually something the actor doesn't understand about the dialogue or situation in the script to make the written dialogue work. The director needs to clarify the intent for the actor.

When to Overlap

Always overlap action. When shooting coverage, always have the actor match the movements from the Master or establishing shots. If the actor has moved in previous setups into or out of a position, it needs to be duplicated. If in the master, an actor sits into a chair, in the close coverage, the actor should start off camera and sit into the shot. If the action is not matched or even overlapped, the editor and ultimately the director, is limited in where the cut into coverage can be made. If the actor has important dialogue that the director wants in a close up, the editor may not be able to make the cut if the action is not overlapped.

Fix it in Post?

Get it right on the set, even if the AD is pushing to move on. There are two phrases a director should distrust when they are heard on the set. The first is "We'll fix it in post," and the other is "Don't worry, it'll cut great." First of all, the "fix" in post will never be as good as getting right on the set. The second is almost a guarantee that there is no way the cut will ever work.

The Cutting Room

Everything I've talked about previously has been intended to help the director give the editor the material and information to assemble an Editor's Cut that, as close as possible, conveys the writer's intent and the director's vision. That being said, the first viewing of an editor's cut may be very disappointing. It will probably feel too long and too slow. Any weaknesses in performance will be exaggerated. There will be cutting patterns that are unexpected. All that's okay. Set aside any thoughts of a different career. Assuming the editor is qualified, there is no reason to want to make a change or worse, cause the editor bodily harm.

First, watch the cut as if you were an audience and try not to anticipate what you're expecting to see. Don't take any notes. There may be ways that the editor has cut a scene that are better than what you expected. Then just watch it again. Watching an Editor's Cut is stressful for both the director and the editor. The disappointment of not seeing the picture you thought you shot can be disheartening. Assuming the editor worked hard to present the best possible cut, the editor is disappointed with the reaction of the director to his work. This may be the first interaction between the two, and it's clearly not the best way to start a professional relationship.

Giving notes to an editor

Start with generally positive feed back. Let the editor know you appreciated the work that has gone into preparing the cut. Appreciation more than praise will set a positive tone. Whether working in the cutting room or giving notes long distance, having a comfortable working relationship is key to good results. Remember editors are creative people who may be sensitive to criticism. However, there is no need to hesitate in giving clear and direct change notes.

Avoid harsh or negative comments but give notes that indicate what is needed. " This scene needs to be paced up" gives the editor direction. "This scene is slow" is a negative remark that doesn't indicate the specific problem. Is it slow cutting or are the actors acting with the proper energy. Tell the editor what you'd like done, not what you don't like. It's hard for the editor to do something positive with a negative comment. By saying what you want, it easier for the editor to find the fix. If an editor has gone in a different direction with a scene than you anticipated, you can start with, "Here is what I had in mind when I shot this." Then you can then tell the editor as clearly as possible how it was envisioned. Just practically speaking, the editor is more likely to work with you and help you realize your vision, if the relationship is positive and respectful.

Diagnostics

What isn't working? Watch each scene and determine as specifically as possible what about the scene needs to change. Are the cuts falling in the right order to best tell the story? Has the editor used the right pieces of coverage, the selected takes and the desired performances or action? Is the pace right?

A producer I know prefers to write editing notes on a copy of the script. Today, cuts are delivered with a running time code starting from the top of the show through to the end. Giving editing notes with "ins and outs" by time code is an exact and specific system. The more specific the understanding of what isn't working, the clearer you can be in giving notes. Even if you plan to work with the editor in the cutting room, it's best to come into the cutting room prepared with notes. Time with the editor is limited. As schedules get tighter, the time can be even less. If with the editor in the cutting room, it's best to come into the cutting room prepared with notes. Time with the editor is limited. As schedules get tighter, the time can be even less. If you are unprepared, the chance of getting bogged down, by not budgeting the time in the cutting room properly, risks not getting the cut you envisioned.

Always be the audience

Trying to keep a "fresh eye" in viewing the cut is difficult and there can be a tendency to over work it. The audience is continually getting new information and needs to process it. When trimming and tightening during editing be careful not to rob the audience of what it may need to fully appreciate the story. Film can be like a relationship. The more intimacy, the more flaws are seen that others wouldn't notice. If there is a mismatch of action on a cut that is not noticed in the first or second viewing, chances are the cut is fine and if it works for the story it shouldn't be changed. Defensive editing to cover perceived weaknesses in coverage or performance can lead to awkward cutting patterns. Be careful that the solutions are not worse than the problem.

Gracious Guest

And finally, directors working in episodic television should always be aware of the show's tone and the shooting and editing styles. Most series producers don't want directors to "reinvent the wheel." The creative people on a series have worked hard to set a tone and a look for the show. It's important to embrace the show's distinctive characteristics and idiom. These parameters should be a stimulation to creativity, rather than a limitation. When working with the editor, be sensitive to what could be the series editing style when making changes. Director should view previous episodes to become familiar with the editing style of the show. If you disregard the general "modus operandi" of the series, it will diminish the chances of being invited back to direct future episodes.

Made in the USA
Lexington, KY
16 March 2014